PYTHON FOR DATA ANALYSIS:

HOW THE PYTHON CODING IS
REVOLUTIONIZING COMPUTER
PROGRAMMING LANGUAGE AND WHAT
YOU NEED TO KNOW ABOUT IT RIGHT
NOW WITH A PYTHON CRASH COURSE
EXPLAINED FOR BEGINNERS.

Table of Contents

Introduction 1

Chapter 1: Will You Migrate from Perl To Python? 9

Chapter 2: Five Important Considerations in Data Science 13

Chapter 3: Introduction to Statistics 21

Chapter 4: Detecting and Treating Outliers 29

Chapter 5: Control Flow Tools 31

Chapter 6: Methods and manipulating the ndarray in NumPy 47

Chapter 7: Data frames 63

Chapter 8: IPython and Jupyter Notebooks 83

Chapter 9: Numpy for Numerical Data Processing 89

Chapter 10: Challenges of Categorical Data 99

Chapter 11: Loading Data, File Formats and Storage 103

Chapter 12: Career Applications 121

Conclusion 131

Introduction

There are going to be a few different parts that come into play when you start to learn how to work with the Python code even with machine learning. You can work with the comments, functions, statements, and more. Let's take a look at some of the basic parts that come with coding in Python so that we can do some of these more complicated things together as we progress through machine learning.

The Comments

The first aspect of the Python coding language that we need to explore is that of comments. There is going to be some point when you are writing out a code where you would like to take a break and explain to others and yourself what took place in the code. This is going to ensure that anyone who sees the code knows what is going on at one point to another. Working with a comment is the way that you would showcase this in your project, and can make it easier for others to know the name of that part, or why you are doing one thing compared to another.

When you would like to add in some comments to the code, you are going to have a unique character that goes in front of your chosen words. This unique code is going to be there to help you tell the computer program that it should skip reading those words and move on to the next part of the code instead. The unique character that you are going to use for this one is the # sign in front of the comments you are writing. When the compiler sees this, it is going to know that you don't want that part of the code to execute at all. It will wait until the next line before it gets started with rereading the code. An example of a comment that you may see in your code would include:

#this is a new comment. Please do not execute in the code.

After you have written out the comment that you want here, and you are done with it, you are then able to hit the return button or enter so that you can write more code that the compiler can execute. You can have the freedom to comment as long or as short as you would like based on what you would need in the code. And you can write in as many of these comments as you would like. It is usually seen as a better option if you keep the comments down to what you need. Otherwise, it makes the code start to look a little bit messy overall. But you can technically add in as many of these comments to your code as you would like.

The Statements

The next part of the code that we need to focus on is the statements. Any time that you are starting with your new code, whether you are working with Python or with some other coding language along the way, you must add these statements inside of the code. This allows the compiler to know what you would like to happen inside. A statement is going to be a unit of code that you would like to send to your interpreter. From there, the interpreter is going to look over the statement and execute it based on the command that you added in.

Any time you decide to write out the code, you can choose how many statements are needed to get the code to work for you. Sometimes, you need to work with one statement in a block of code, and other times, you will want to have more than one. As long as you can remember that the statements should be kept in the brackets of your code, it is fine to make the statement as long as you would like, and include as many statements as you would like.

When you are ready to write your code and add in at least one statement to your code, you would then need to send it over so that the interpreter can handle it all. As long as the interpreter can understand the statements that you are trying to write out, it is going to execute your command. The results of that statement are going to show up on the screen. If you notice that you write out your code and something doesn't seem to show up in it the right way, then you need to go back through the code and check whether they are written the right way or not.

Now, this all may sound like a lot of information, but there is a way to minimize the confusion and ensure that it can make more sense to you. Let's take a look at some examples of how this is all going to work for you.

x = 56

Name = John Doe

z = 10

print(x)

print(Name)

print(z)

When you send this over to the interpreter, the results that should show up on the screen are:

56

John Doe

10

It is as simple as that. Open up Python, and give it a try to see how easy it is to get a few things to show up in your interpreter.

The Variables

The next things we consider inside our Python codes are the variables. These variables are important to learn about because they are the part that will store your code in the right places so you can pull them up later on. This means that if you do this process in the right way, the variables are going to be found inside the right spot of the memory in the computer. The data in the code will help determine which spots of the memory these points will be stored on, but this makes it easier for you to find the information when it is time to run the code.

The first thing that we need to focus on here is to make sure that the variable has a value assigned to it. If there is a variable without a value, then the variable won't have anything to save and store. If the variable is given a good value from the start, then it will behave the way you are expecting when you execute the program.

When it comes to your Python code, there are going to be three types of variables that you can choose from. They are all important and will have their place to work. But you have to choose the right one based on the value that you would like to attach to that variable. The main variables that are available for you with Python are going to include:

1. Float: This is going to be an integer variable that includes numbers like 3.14

2. String: This is going to be one of those statements that you would write out. You can add in any phrase that you would like to this one.

3. Whole number: This is going to be any of the other numbers that you would want to use, ones that are not going to contain a decimal.

When you are trying to work with the variables in your program, you won't have to go through and make a declaration to make sure the memory space is available. This is something that Python can do for you automatically, as soon as a value is assigned to a variable. If you would like to make sure that this is happening in your code and avoid some of the surprises along the way, you need to double check that the equal sign, the sign of giving a variable value is in the right place. An excellent example of how this is going to look when you write out a code includes the following

x = 12#this is an example of an integer assignment

pi = 3.14#this is an example of a floating point assignment

customer name = John Doe #this is an example of a string assignment

In some instances, you may need to have one variable with two or more values attached to it. There are certain times when you won't be able to avoid this and need to make it happen. The good news is that you can work with the same procedure discussed above to make this happen, you need to make sure that there is an equal sign to each part so that the compiler knows how to assign everything. So, when you want to do this, you would want to write out something like a = b = c = 1.

The Keywords

Any time that you are using the Python language, like what we find in other coding languages as well, you are going to come across some words that are reserved as commands in the code, and these are going to be known as keywords. You need to be careful about the way you use these because they are there to tell the program some commands, and how you would like it to behave. You don't want to bring these and use them in any other place outside of a particular command.

If you do misuse these keywords, it is going to cause some confusion inside the code. The interpreter isn't going to know what to do, and the computer may get stalled in what it needs to do. As we go through this guidebook some more and develop a few Python codes for machine learning, we will start to recognize some of the most common keywords that you need to watch out for.

Naming Your Identifiers

The next thing that we need to focus on is how to name all of the identifiers. You need to do this in a way that makes sense, and will not confuse the computer along the way. Any time that you are writing out a particular code in Python, you are going to have at least a few identifiers that show up. Some of the most common of these identifiers are going to including classes, entities, variables, and functions.

At one point or another, you will need to name out the identifiers so that they are more likely to work in the way that they should and make it easier for the compiler to pull them up when it is time to execute the code. No matter which of the four identifiers that you use, the rules for naming are going to be the same, which can make it easier when you get started. Some of the rules you should remember when naming your identifiers include:

Any time that you are using letters, it is fine to use either upper case or lower case, and a combination of both is fine as well. You can also add in numbers, symbols, and an underscore to the name. Any combination of these are acceptable, make sure that there are no spaces between the characters of the name.

Never start the name of one of your identifiers with a number. This means that writing out the name of 4babies would result in an error on your computer. However, it is acceptable to name an identifier "fourbabies" if you would like.

The identifier should never be one of the Python keywords, and the keyword should not appear in the name at all.

Now, if you are trying to go through and write out a few of your codes along the way, and you don't follow all of the rules that are above, you will confuse the compiler, and it will send you an error message to let you know something is wrong. The error will then be on your computer, and the program will close out because it doesn't know how to proceed. This is something that you don't want to happen, so be careful when naming these identifiers.

Another thing to remember with these identifiers and naming them is that you want to make sure that you are picking out names that are ready for you to remember. And picking out names that are easy to understand and read will make it easier if another programmer comes in, and is trying to look through the code as well.

What Else Do I Need to Know About the Python Coding Language?

The Python coding language is often considered to be one of the best languages for programming by the experts, and this is even truer if you are someone who has never worked with coding in the past. This language is simple, it has plenty of power, and there are a lot of the tools and the resources that are needed to help you work on your project, even if that project has to do with machine learning. While there are other options that you can use with machine learning, those are often a bit more difficult to work with, and Python is often the better choice.

One thing that you will like when you first start working with the Python language is that the whole thing is based on the English language. What this means is that you will recognize the words and what they mean, rather than trying to guess. And even though it is a language that is great for beginners who have never worked with coding before, it is going to be strong enough to work with machine learning and any other topic that you would like.

As someone ready to learn and get started with the Python language, you will notice that it has a nice big library available that you can utilize when you are coding. And this library is going to have the tools and the resources that you need, making it easier for beginners and experts alike to write out any code that they need.

Chapter 1: Will You Migrate from Perl To Python?

Python and Perl are advanced, open source, multipurpose, interpreted languages for high-ranking programming. Nonetheless, figures on various websites show that Python is popular more than Perl. Thus, by switching Perl to Python, a software developer could improve career prospects.

No additional time or effort, beginners can learn more and use Python. Nevertheless, you must not move into a new programming language because of its success and use. If you decide to move from Perl to Python, remember the main differences between the two languages.

12 points Perl was originally intended to be a scripting language to promote the creation of reports from Perl to Python 1. It requires text storage capabilities. On the other hand, Python is known as a language for hobby programming. It was developed to help developers build fast, readable and reusable software applications. The function and quality of both programming languages also vary.

2) Rules of Syntax Several other Python and Perl Rules have been influenced by other languages. Perl uses C, shell scripts, sed, AWK, and Lisp programming languages. The programming features in Python are also Lisp-like. Nonetheless, Python is extremely popular with modern languages through the simple rules of syntax. In addition to being user friendly, the syntax rules of Python allow programmers to except several coded concepts that are not readable.

(3) The Perl Language Family is a member of the highly skilled Perl 5 and Perl 6 language family. Compatible with Perl versions 5 and 6. By adding time, the programmer can easily move from Perl 5 to Perl 6. With two different versions, take Python 2 and Python 2. But the two versions of

Python are incompatible. Therefore, the developer will choose from two different language versions of the programming.

4) Python helps programmers to express ideas without any longer code lines. Yet programmers must carry out tasks in a specific, simple way to achieve performance. Nonetheless, Perl lets programmers perform one function in a number of different ways and achieve the same results. Many programmers think Perl would be better than Python. The various ways in which the same result can be obtained, however, also make it difficult to hold the code written in Perl.

5) The Perl Web Scripts have been designed originally for UNIX. Many programmers use Perl to use his integrated text processing capabilities as a scripting language. But the majority of web developers agree that Perl is lighter than other languages. Developers of web applications often use Python. Nevertheless, the ability for web development is not included. The developers therefore need to use frameworks and tools to efficiently and quickly write Web applications in Python.

6) Frameworks for Web Application Several developers are now using different framing frameworks and functions to make web applications reactive and effective. Perl's web programmers can choose from different frameworks: Catalyst, Dancer, Mojolicious, Poet, Interchange, Jifty and Gantry. Web developers can also use a variety of Python web frames including Django, Flask, Pyramid, Bottle and Cherrypy. Nonetheless, the configurations of Python's page are much lower than the system configuration of Perl.

7) This language is therefore used to build software applications. Perl is used widely for modeling graphics and networking, system management, accounting and biometric applications. Nevertheless, Python does have a robust standard library that makes building web applications, scientific

computing, creating big data solutions and artificial intelligence tasks easier. Developers tend to use Python to develop special software applications that are mission-critical.

8) There has been a number of studies showing that Python is less sluggish than other languages such as Java and C++. Programmers are also exploring ways to improve the speed at which Python code is executed. Most developers often replace default Python runtime with the custom framework for faster running of Python applications. Most schedulers believe Perl is quicker than Python. Most programmers use Perl to improve the speed of web applications and the user experience in scripting languages.

The big data is a key advancement in app development. 9) Structured data analyze. Most companies now develop specialized technology to capture, store and analyze large quantities of unstructured ordered data. Perl's PDL allows developers to analyze large amounts of data. Perl's integrated text processing system makes analyzing large quantities of structured information easier and quicker. Nonetheless, Python is usually used by data analysis programmers. Developers can use common Python libraries such as Numpy to quickly and efficiently store and analyze large volumes of data.

10) Java is currently one of the most used desktop, web and phone programming languages. Just like Perl, Java Virtual Machine (JVM) is a Python interface. Now programmers can use powerful Java APIs and artifacts to write Python Code in JVM instead of running smoothly. Interoperability helps software developers to target the generic Java platform when writing Java rather than Python code.

11) Perl and Python are specialized object-oriented programming. Python implements better than Perl the dynamic object-oriented languages of

programming. For Perl, programmers need to use packages rather than classes when writing code. Programmers from Python can use classes and objects to write high-quality, modular code. It is difficult for many programmers to maintain code in Perl while they write object-oriented code. Nevertheless, Perl helps programmers to carry out a variety of tasks with a liner.

12) The ability to process text Like Python, Perl has been developed for text processing. For the development of reports, most programmers use Perl. Perl allows programmers to fit, substitute and override regex and string comparison operations. But for error handling and I / O operations, the programmers do not need to type additional code. Many programmers therefore prefer Perl to Python for developing applications for the storage or reporting of text information.

Many developers of code usually favor Python over Perl. Nonetheless, other applications are currently more widely available–Java, C, C++ and C #–than Perl and Python. Python has its own drawbacks, as has other software. Using Python frameworks for programming, for instance, when writing applications. Therefore, consider both languages before switching from Perl to Python, their advantages and disadvantages.

Chapter 2: Five Important Considerations in Data Science

Data science is growing very prominently as a tool of strategic business. It has been found out in a study by Deloitte that many organizations are looking to triple their team of data scientists within the next 24 months. With the current implementations of GDPR and privacy being under scrutiny more than ever, data scientists have made it important to model and process data in a responsible manner. The following five considerations are what data scientists are looking at in the months to come.

- Explainability and Transparency

- Version Control

- Data as the new IP

- Data Bias

- Data Aggregation

Explainability and transparency

May 2016 saw the introduction of General Data Protection Regulation (GDPR), which paved a change in the manner global organizations would collect, manage and process data of people belonging to the European Union. This resulted in an impact in the field of data science as it made it important to think about what kind of data can be used by data science for its modeling purposes and how transparent would the models need to be. As per GDPR compliance an organization should be able to justify how they arrived at a decision that was based on data models. This implies that any organization must secure all the data that they have on a customer and should have sufficient consent from the customer if they want to use that data. It is also expected that in the coming years, regulations around ePrivacy could get a lot harsher which will have an impact on how data can be used. Data architecture will be the next real challenge for data scientists such that it stays in compliance with the regulations made by the law makers.

Version Control

Version control for data is closely associated with GDPR and ePrivacy. Changes being made to software and data by you or other people working on the project is very critical to the project. Why is this important? This is really important if you are building models that goes through build change frequently or partially until it reaches the latest build, it is important to store both historic and current builds of the data in the event of an audit.

This holds true in the case where you are running frequent iterations on development of models. Model development is a process that goes through iterations, wherein new packages and techniques are being made available with each iteration. Business should be attentive to their complete suite of models and not just the new models. Versioning should be given importance and implemented so as to be in compliance at all given times. Whether you are a person who makes changes and maintains them manually, or you use version control software like Git, or you are outsourcing version control, you need to ensure that version control is your priority as a data scientist. Failing to do so will put you and your work at risk and can result in the wrath of an Information Commissioner who may even fine you heavily.

Data as the new IP

There is a theory that data is becoming the new IP because along with the code in a software, data is as important now while creating models that are proprietary. The standard of using open source software is growing and computer resources are therefore becoming more affordable. This means that many more enterprises can now build software without a very high budget. The availability of quality and volume in training data is what differentiates models. This holds true for both industries which are just adapting to the new market and are generally slow and static where the data is sparse, and fast-moving industries where data is retrained frequently. If you look at data giants like Google and Amazon, you will understand that training data is quickly becoming an intellectual property and something that gives one company a competitive advantage over another.

Data bias

Model retraining using automation is all well and good. There is a problem, however, which is that of human bias, a problem that is supposed to be eliminated using algorithms and machine learning. Human bias can be passed to a machine when a machine is being trained in the event that the data being fed to the machine contains traces of a bias. For example, consider a finance industry. If the data being fed is biased, the results may end up offending the fair lending act known as the Equal Credit Opportunity Act. As we have learned from the GDPR act, a customer has the right to know about how a decision was reached; if a loan was rejected, and if this decision was reached due to a bias of data, the case could become difficult to be justified to the customer. We have seen a number of data sets where speech recognition models could not recognize regional accents and image recognition models returned results that were racist in nature, all because the data used to train the models was skewed and biased in nature.

Data Aggregation

GDPR states that anonymity should be ensured by aggregating customer data to a group size that is specific in nature. This does feel like something that would put restrictions on maintaining data but we could also look at it as an opportunity to put more creativity into the thought process that goes into building models and how they would be of benefit to the consumer. Innovation in techniques in clustering and feature generation of data would mean that we will be able to understand and recognize patterns in data and information that were not seen previously. Instead of just trying to comply with GDPR, we could use this as an opportunity to create new models and techniques that will be more customer centric.

Data science has reached a state of its development cycle that is very interesting. There is something new happening every day and newer possibilities are being introduced that can be afforded by the discipline. We should also focus on how we can appreciate privacy of data and that it is the responsibility of data scientists to train machines to respect the data of consumers whose data is being used.

Ten Platforms to be Used in the Field of Data Science

The reaction between the huge volume of data that is available to organizations and how they can put it to use in their decision making such that the organization benefits from this data is what resulted in the need for data science in today's world. The absence of proper tools is all that stands as an obstacle to determine the value that all this information and data has in determining the economic and social value of this data for an organization. Data science came into existence to fill this void of tools to analyze and use this huge set of data. For a business to grow at a constant and good rate, for it to develop, inputs are required which will allow the business to manufacture and produce a product that is required by the consumer. Data science teams come into the picture to develop these specific needs of a growing business. When the general population gives intimate feedback to the models built by a data science team, you can say that their purpose is achieved. If the population were not to work with the models that a data science team creates, thee business may not be able to tackle the issue of growth that the special data science team is battling with.

There are a few platforms available that serve the needs of developing models in data science and allow integration of coding languages to serve the same purpose. Models developed for data science are usually unpredictable and require proper coding knowledge and hardware that support it. To use the data models in data science, data scientists usually deploy multiple machines that are powerful enough and the data processing is simultaneously distributed between all these machines. The platforms do not support programming languages such that one can code in the platform but allow the models to be passed as inputs in python, R, or SAS which can execute the data model code. They, therefore work as a system together with the data models by creating a group in data science. Let us have a look at all the platforms that are available to the field of data science that support the use of analytics code and are universally accepted across the world.

Matlab

When it comes to analytics of entities such as cloud processing, machine learning, neural systems, image processing and so on, MATLAB is the go-to software for many data scientists which is a platform that is very simple and easy to understand and get a grasp on. Huge amounts of data coming from multiple sources can be analyzed with the help of MATLAB. The versatile nature of MATLAB gives it a range from telematics, sensor analytics, all the way to predictive analysis. With the help of MATLAB, data from various sources such as web content, video, images, sound, record frameworks, IoT gadgets, etc. can all be analyzed. MATLAB offers a 1-month free trial and provides annual licenses beginning from USD 820 per year.

TIBCO Statistica

Multiple enterprises deploy TIBO Statistica to understand and solve their numerous issues that are unpredictable in nature. The platform allows users to assemble different models built by them allowing for refreshed learning, analytical procedures, artificial intelligence, and so on. With the help of TIBCO Statistica, one can create complex level of algorithms such as clustering, neural systems, machine learning, all which are accessible via a few nodes.

Alteryx Analytics

A California based software company is the creator of Alteryx Analytics. Business intelligence and predictive analytics products are the primary offerings of this software company that are used for processes related to data science and analytics. The annual membership starts from USD 3995.00 per year and their cloud-based software suite starts at a pricing of USD 1950.00 per year. Data giants like Amazon Web Services, Microsoft, Tableau and Qlik are partners with Asteryx Analytics.

RapidMiner Studio

RapidMiner Studio is a software that is considered to be a visual workflow designer. A tool that helps with processes such as data preparation, machine learning, text mining and predictive analytics, it was specifically developed to help make the lives of data scientists easy. Using the RapidMiner Turbo prep, data scientists can do pivots, take charge of transforming data as well as blend data collected from various sources. All these transactions surprisingly can be processes using a minimal number of clicks.

Databricks Unified Analytics Platform

The creators of Apache Spark created the Databricks Unified Analytics Platform. It provides shared notepads and an environment where users can coordinate to tackle and work with a majority of tasks that fall under analytical procedures. Data scientists can create applications working on artificial intelligence and also create new models consistently. The software is available as a trial for a 14-day period.

Anaconda

With a total number of over seven million users all over the world, Anaconda is a software that is free and open source. Anaconda Distribution and Anaconda Enterprise are the most popular products available from this open source package. The Anaconda distribution empowers data scientists with a platform and environment that supports around 2000 data bundles in the programming suite of Python and R language for Data Science.

H2O

Used by industries such as finance, healthcare, retail, manufacturing, telco, etc. H2O brags of a user base of 155,000 users in over 14000 organizations worldwide. Driverless AI, which is one of the tools offered by H2O, made it to the winner's list of the 2018 InfoWorld Technology Awards. Multi million-dollar organizations such as PayPal, Dun and Bradstreet, Cisco, and a few more businesses working in assembly use H2O packages very prominently.

KNIME Analytics Platform

The KNIME Analytics Platform is a software that is open source again. Machine learning algorithms and advanced predictive algorithms that use end-to-end workflow in data science are powered by the KNIME Analytics Platform. This software makes it convenient to retrieve data from sources such as Google, Azure, Twitter and Amazon Web Services S3 buckets.

R-Studio

R programming language clients utilize the R-Studio tool as an Integrated Development Environment. The R-Studio platform is very intelligent and furthermore contains bundles that are built-in, which can be used for graphics and computing data that is statistical in nature. The R-Studio platform is supported by all major operating systems such as Windows, Linux and MAC.

Cloudera Data Science Workbench

Among all the platforms that are available to data scientists, software engineers and programming specialists in the world today, Cloudera Data Science Workbench is the most loved platform by all. The tool contains the latest and most updated libraries scripted in languages such as Python, Scala and R, which can be utilized by end users and data scientists. Data scientists and users have the liberty to develop and create their machine learning models with just a few clicks and hauls which is very comfortable and convenient as compared to all other available platforms.

Chapter 3: Introduction to Statistics

Statistics is the mathematical science of data. It is a practice by which data is collected, observed, and analyzed in order to infer meaning and examine quantifiable relationships between different variables. Machine learning is a form of inferential statistics, meaning that by examining the relationship between variables, we should be able to come up with predictions for new variables.

Statistics is used in a wide variety of disciplines. It's used in biology to study and examines animal and plant life. It has wide applications in the business world from making stock market forecasts to analyzing consumer behavior. Economists use statistics to explain quantifiable patterns in world markets. In medicine, statistics can be used to improve the way that doctors and disease specialists look at the spread and prevention of disease.

Statistics make up the core of machine learning. If you aren't willing to dive into statistics, then machine learning isn't for you. Machine learning uses statistical algorithms to help computers learn. Machine learning is all about the tracking of data and how computers can use data to improve themselves.

There are two types of statistics which are relevant to this book. The first one is descriptive analysis, which you might use during the beginning of your modeling process to look for indicators in your data. But most of what we do in machine learning falls into a different category called predictive analysis.

Key term; Descriptive analysis. The descriptive analysis helps us examine we are right now. Looking at our current situation in context to the past and seeing why things are the way they are. Why do some things sell better than others? What trends are we seeing in products currently on the market?

Key term; Predictive analysis. Predictive analysis helps us to see and understand what will happen in the future based on indicators that are currently present. When we are using machine learning for predictive analysis, it's important for us to stay current and continue to feed the model new data. What trends should we be on the lookout for?

Machine learning is just another way to understand the data that is around us and to help us understand our present and predict the future. But it requires data from the past and present so that we can find trends and see where they might lead.

Within statistics, there are two over-arching categories of data that we will use, and all our data will fall into one category or the other somehow.

The first category is *quantitative data.* Quantitative data is data that can be measured with a numerical value. Some examples of quantitative data include height, income, or the square footage of a house. All these variables can be measured by some number, which makes them quantitative.

The second category is *qualitative data.* Qualitative data is data where the variables are assigned to categories or classes. Examples of qualitative data would include someone's gender, blood type, or whether a piece of real estate has a pool or not. This data can be sorted by its identity and is non-numerical. Therefore it is qualitative.

Quantitative data can either be discrete or continuous. If we have a data set where there is a variable recording the number of patients that a hospital had last year, this would be considered discrete. Discrete variables have a finite amount of values that they can have, and they are always whole numbers. It would be impossible to have half a patient or a percentage of a patient. Therefore this variable is discrete.

Data can also be continuous. An example of continuous data would be a variable for income. Income can take on half values, and there is a virtually infinite amount of possibilities for the value of income in data.

Some other important terms to remember are the mean, median, and mode. You will often hear these three things referred to in this book when we are talking about regressions. These are all different measures of central tendency. The mean is our average value for data. If we have a variable for a person's age, we will find the mean of age by adding all the ages together and then dividing by the number of respondents in a data set.

The *median* is the value in the middle of the dataset. If you took all the responses for age and found the response that was in the exact middle of a sorted list of responses, then this would be your median.

The *mode* is the response that occurs the most frequently. If we took a sample of eleven people's ages and found that the ages were 19, 19, 20, 21, 22, 22, 22, 23, 24, 24, 25 then the mode would be 22, because it occurs the most frequently in this sample. The median would also be 22 because it happens to be in the middle of this sorted list of responses.

When you are making a statistical model, there are many important terms that have to do with the accuracy of our models. These are different kinds of prediction errors that can occur when we are creating statistic models. Ideally, we'd like to minimize the prevalence of bias and variance in our models. They will always be present, and as a data scientist, you will have to find the right balance of bias and variance in your models, whether that's by choosing different data or using different types of models. There are many ways to reduce variance and bias within a model, dependent on what you are trying to do with the data. By trying to reduce these with the wrong approach, you run the risk of overfitting or underfitting your model. When your model is *bias*, it means that the average difference between your predictions and the actual values is very high.

Variance is how to spread out our predicted data points are. Usually, the variance is a result of overfitting to the sample data we used to create the model. It doesn't do very well at predicting the outcome of new variables.

There will always be some level of error in your models. It's a fact of life that no matter how good you are at predicting something, there is always some random or nonrandom variation in the universe that will make your prediction slightly off from the true outcome.

I've created a visual example of four bullseye targets to help illustrate the difference between models suffering from high bias and variance. In this instance, the center of the bullseye represents the true value that our model is trying to predict. The top left corner is the ideal model. Notice that all our predicted data points are falling right on the bullseye. This model is quite accurate and places our predicted data points all around the true value. This is because of low variance; a lack of 'spread out' data points, and low bias; underfitting that skews our results.

In the top right target, the model is suffering from high variance. You can see that our data points are clustered around the bullseye. Unfortunately, the average distance between the predicted values and the bullseye is high due to high variance.

In the bottom left target, the model didn't suffer much from high variance. The average distance between the predicted data points is low, but they aren't clustered around the bullseye but slightly off it as a result of high bias. This is probably the result of too little training data, which means that the model doesn't perform well when it gets introduced to new data.

The bottom right model suffers from both high variance and high bias. In this worst-case scenario, the model is very inaccurate because the average distance between predicted data points and the true value is high, and the predicted data points are skewed.

Variance can be caused by a significant degree of correlation between variables. If you use too many independent variables, this can also be a cause of the high variance. Sometimes, if the variance is too high, we can combat that by allowing a small amount of bias in the model. This is known as regularization. We'll cover that a little later.

In statistics, the *population* is the group of people or the set of data you are trying to analyze. The *sample* is the subgroup of that population, whose data you use to create your model. The *parameters* are the characteristic of the variables of the population that you are trying to identify and make predictions from in your model.

Descriptive statistics is the use of data to examine a population. Typically, descriptive statistics involve the mean or average, mode, media, size, correlation. Machine learning falls into the category of inferential statistics because we are using the data to find patterns and relations but also to make predictions based on this information. Inferential statistics, or descriptive stats, is using the characteristics of your population to make predictions. This is where your regression models and classification models will come in. When we infer something, we make a logical deduction about a population-based and the knowledge we are given.

When you are looking at data, you should also take note of the *distribution*. This is how the data is spread out on our graph. It shows the frequency of values of our data and how they appear in conjunction with one another.

We use our variance to find the standard *deviation*. Standard deviation is the average of the distances between the predicted data points and the real data points on a regression or prediction model.

We must also be sure to be aware of models that suffer from overfitting and underfitting. An overfitted model is good at predicting outcomes using the training data, but when you introduce new data, then it struggles. It's like a model that memorizes instead of learns. It can happen if you don't use random data in your training sample.

Underfitting describes a model that is too simple, and it doesn't examine any significant data patterns. It may do a good job of predicting, but the variables and parameters aren't specific enough to give us any meaningful insights if you don't have enough training data, your model could be under fitted.

One of the most commonly made mistakes when people are looking at data, is confusing correlation with causation. If I told you that every person who committed a murder last year bought eggs every week, I couldn't claim that people who buy eggs are murderers. Maybe looking at my data, I see a rise in people buying milk, as well as a rise in teen pregnancy. Would I be able to claim that there is an association between people drinking a lot of milk and teen pregnancy? Or teenagers getting pregnant caused people to buy more milk.

This is the difference between correlation and causation. Sometimes the data shows trends that seem like they are related. When two events are correlated, it means that they seem to have a relationship because they move along the graph at a similar trajectory, and during a similar space in time. Whereas causation means that the relationship between the two events involves one event causing another.

In order to imply that two things have a causal relationship, a few criteria need to be met. The first is covariation. The causal variable, and the event, it is supposed to have caused the need to be covarying, meaning that a change in one lead to a change in the other.

The second criterion that needs to be met is that the causal event needs to occur before the event it is supposed to have caused. For an event to be considered causal, it must come first.

Third, the data scientist must control for outside factors. In order to make a strong case that one thing causes another; you need to be able to present evidence that the other variables of the event are not the true cause. If the causal variable still creates the effect, even when other variables are considered, then you can claim there is a causal relationship.

Chapter 4: Detecting and Treating Outliers

Examples lie at the heart of learning from a data process. If we introduce faulty data that is incomplete, we won't be able to accommodate new data to the result. This will lead to erroneous machine learning algorithms that will cause distorted results. When we have a data point deviation when compared to other data points, we call it an outlier. Here are the main causes that lead to the creation of an outlier. Focus on them, because it's important to understand the source of the problem in order to know how to fix it.

1. The first scenario is that of an outlier that appears as a rare occurrence. In this case, the data is a sample of the original data distribution and the process is identical for all the data points, but the outlier is marked as unsuitable because of its rarity. When this scenario is encountered, the outlier is simply removed from the dataset.

2. In the second scenario, we have an outlier that is a usual occurrence. When you encounter too many similar situations, there is a high possibility of having an error that had an effect on how the sample was generated. When the focus on the machine learning algorithm should be generalization, the learning algorithm in this scenario will learn from a superfluous distribution that is not the focus. Again, the outlier needs to be removed when such a situation is found.

3. The third scenario is the case of a data point that is an obvious error. Usually, there's a data entry mistake that lead to the modification of the original value and changed it to something inconsistent. In this case, the value should be removed and then treated as if it's randomly missing. It is common to replace this value with an average, however, if it's difficult to execute this path, the outlier should simply be removed.

The first step in learning which scenario describes the type of the outlier is to detect all outliers and find their location. There are basically two methods to achieve this. You can analyze every singular variable at the same time, or multiple variables. These methods are referred to as univariate and multivariate. One of the most common univariate method you already encountered in an early example, and that is the visualization with the help of a Boxplot.

When a data scientist uses this method, they need to keep in mind that outliers can be identified as extreme values. For example, if you are looking at a data description, there might be an outlier if the observation is smaller than 25% - the difference between the 75% and 25% values * 1.5. Similarly, this possibility also exists if you encounter an observation greater than 75% + the difference between the 75% and 25% values* 1.5. This can easily be detected when looking at a boxplot. Another example is when you are observing Z-scores. Generally, if you encounter a value greater than 3, you can suspect it to be an outlier.

The univariate method can expose many outliers, but not all of them. It will only expose the outliers that are represented by extreme values. Those that are a combination of values in several variables will escape this method of inspection. This is what data scientists refer to as multivariate outliers. They work because they allow us to observe plots of isolated data points.

Validation Metrics

In order to determine how close, you are to your original objective, you have to use a scoring function. These are used to evaluate the performance of your data system by dealing with binary classification, regression, or a multi-label classification. Let's discuss and examine some of the functions to understand how to use them in machine learning.

Chapter 5: Control Flow Tools

The next thing that we can take a look at is some of the control flow tools that are available. There are a lot of different parts that you are able to add into your code to make sure that it can handle decisions, that you can deal with any errors that show up, and ensure that the program is going to work the way that you would like. Some of the different control flow tools that you can work with and can help you learn some of the basics of coding in Python include:

Comparison Operators

There are a lot of different types of operators that you are able to use based on what you would like to see happen in your code. The most common types of operators are going to be the arithmetic operators that allow you to add and subtract different parts of your code together. But the comparison operators can be an important part of the code. The comparison operators are going to make it possible to take at least two parts of the code and compare them to one another. You will have to use what is known as the Boolean expressions for this because you are going to get an answer that either says true or false. The parts of the code that you are comparing, for example, are either going to be the same, so true, or they will be different, which is false. There are a few operators that you will be able to work with that fit under the term of comparison operators which include:

- (>=): this one means to check if the left-hand operand is greater than or equal to the value of the one on the right.

- (<=): this one means to check if the value of the left-hand operand is less than or equal to the one on the right.

- (>): this one means to check whether the values of the left side are greater than the value on the right side of the code.

- (<): this one means to check whether the values of the left side are less than the values that are on the right side.

- (!=): this is the **not equal to** operator.

- (==): this one is **the equal to** operator.

The if statements

Conditional statements are going to be an important part of your code as well. These allow the program to make decisions, based on the conditions that you set. There are three different types of conditional statements that you are able to work with including the if statement, the if-else statement, and the elif statement. All of these are going to work in a similar manner, but it depends on how you would like the program to behave and what you want it to do.

Let's start with the if statement. This is the most basic out of the three, and it is not used as often because it missed on out a few things that you need. With this option, the user puts in an input that is either true or false based on the conditions that you set. If the answer is true, then your code will proceed. If the answer is false, then the code is going to stop because there is nothing there. An example of how this is going to work as code is to put the following code into your compiler and execute it:

```
age = int(input("Enter your age:"))

if (age <=18):

print("You are not eligible for voting, try next election!")

print("Program ends")
```

Then we need to take a look at the if-else statements. These follow the same idea that we saw with the if statements but takes it a bit further to handle what the user puts in, no matter the answer. You can keep it simple, with one result if the answer is true and another if it is false. Or you can allow for a range of answers, with a catch-all to catch any of the answers that you didn't include. For example, if you wanted the user to pick out their favorite color, you may include five color choices in the if-else statement, and then use the catch-all, or the else part of the code, to catch any other color the user would like to use.

We will start with a basic if-else statement, going off the idea that we did in the code above. This one will catch the age of the user whether they are younger than 18 or above. The code that you can use to have this happen includes:

```
age = int(input("Enter your age:"))

if (age <=18):
```

print("You are not eligible for voting, try next election!")

else

print("Congratulations! You are eligible to vote. Check out your local polling station to find out more information!)

print("Program ends")

And the third option that you are able to work with will be the elif statement. These can be compared to the menu option that you would see with a game. The user will be able to choose from a specific number of options, and then the code will proceed from there. The user can not just put in what they want; they have to choose one of the options that are given for the elif statement to work the way that you want.

Let's look at an example of how this will work. We are going to make our own menu that includes options for the user to chose which type of pizza they would like to eat. You can type in the following code to help you get this done:

Print("Let's enjoy a Pizza! Ok, let's go inside Pizzahut!")

print("Waiter, Please select Pizza of your choice from the menu")

pizzachoice = int(input("Please enter your choice of Pizza:"))

if pizzachoice == 1:

print('I want to enjoy a pizza napoletana')

```
elif pizzachoice == 2:

print('I want to enjoy a pizza rustica')

elif pizzachoice == 3:

print('I want to enjoy a pizza capricciosa')

else:

print("Sorry, I do not want any of the listed pizzas, please bring a Coca
Cola for me.")
```

Exceptions

Exceptions are a unique thing that you are able to add into your code. These are going to either be raised as a personal exception based on how things work in your particular code, or they could be a specific exception that Python raises because the user did something that is not allowed. A good example of this is when the user tries to divide by zero, or they try to use the wrong name, or the wrong spelling, to bring out a variable or a function later on.

Knowing how to raise these exceptions can be important when you are trying to work on your code. There is a lot that goes into them, but knowing how these work can give you some more control over the codes that you are writing, and can help you learn how to anticipate when these are going to show up, while also determining how you would like to handle them.

There is a lot that you are able to do when it comes to exceptions in your code, but we are going to focus on the meat of it and look at how you can raise some of your own exceptions. The basic code that we are going to be able to work with that ensures that you are able to deal with an error that shows up while making sure that you can leave a personalized message to the user so they know what they are aware of what problem is going on so they can fix it includes:

```
x = 10

y = 0

result = 0

try:

result = x/y


    print(result)

except ZeroDivisionError:

print("You are trying to divide by zero.")
```

You could choose to work on the code and not add in this personalized message, but this makes it easier. Most of the users you are going to deal with on your program are not going to be coders, and they will not understand what the long and drawn out error message is all about. With that in mind, being able to write it out and explain what is going on and how the user can fix it, like with the example above, can make things a bit easier on everyone.

The Inheritances

It is also important that we take a look at how some of these inheritances are going to work in the code that you work with. Working with an inheritance is a great way for you to have a chance to enhance a lot of the codes that can be created in Python. These inheritances are going to cut down on a lot of the time it takes to get things done while making sure that the code looks better and can run properly. Inheritances are going to be something that is new and unique to OOP languages so having them available in Python can be a nice perk.

Basically, when you decide to work with these inheritances, you will be able to take the first part of the code that you have, which we are going to call the parent code, and then move it down so you can make some changes to it, without messing with the original code that you were writing. You can do this without having anything change with the parent code while reusing and changing up the parts that you would like from the parent code.

To help us see how this kind of inheritance is going to work for us, we need to take a look at some of the code that you are going to be able to rely on when doing Python. Some example of coding that works well for this includes the following below:

```python
#Example of inheritance

#base class

class Student(object):

def __init__(self, name, rollno):

self.name = name

self.rollno = rollno

#Graduate class inherits or derived from Student class

class GraduateStudent(Student):

def __init__(self, name, rollno, graduate):

Student __init__(self, name, rollno)

self.graduate = graduate
def DisplayGraduateStudent(self):

print"Student Name:", self.name)

print("Student Rollno:", self.rollno)

print("Study Group:", self.graduate)
```

#Post Graduate class inherits from Student class

```python
class PostGraduate(Student):

def__init__(self, name, rollno, postgrad):

Student__init__(self, name, rollno)

self.postgrad = postgrad
def DisplayPostGraduateStudent(self):

print("Student Name:", self.name)

print("Student Rollno:", self.rollno)

print("Study Group:", self.postgrad)
#instantiate from Graduate and PostGraduate classes

objGradStudent = GraduateStudent("Mainu", 1, "MS-Mathematics")

objPostGradStudent = PostGraduate("Shainu", 2, "MS-CS")


        objPostGradStudent.DisplayPostGraduateStudent()
```

When you type this into your interpreter, you are going to get the results:

('Student Name:', 'Mainu')

('Student Rollno:', 1)

('Student Group:', 'MSC-Mathematics')

('Student Name:', 'Shainu')

('Student Rollno:', 2)

('Student Group:', 'MSC-CS')

Functions

The next part of the code that we need to take a quick look at is going to be the Python functions. These functions are simply just a set of expressions and can be called statements in some cases, and are either going to be anonymous or have a name depending on what the programmer would like. These functions are going to be some of the objects that belong to the first class, which means that there aren't going to necessarily be a ton of restrictions on what you can use these for in the code.

With this said, you will find that there is a lot of diversity that comes with the functions and you are able to work with a lot of attributes to make these run. A few of the different attributes that work well with the Python functions will include:

- __doc__: This is going to return the docstring of the function that you are requesting.

- Func_default: This one is going to return a tuple of the values of your default argument.

- Func_globals: This one will return a reference that points to the dictionary holding the global variables for that function.

- Func_dict: This one is responsible for returning the namespace that will support the attributes for all your arbitrary functions.

- Func_closure: This will return to you a tuple of all the cells that hold the bindings for the free variables inside of the function.

The Loops

Loops are another important part of the code that we need to spend some time on. These are basically going to be a helpful part that cuts down on the actual number of lines of code that you need to write out at a time. If there is something in your code that you need to have repeated over again at least a few times, such as a chart or a table that you want to make, then the loop will come in and handle this for you. It saves time it makes the code look better and helps you to not have to write out as many lines of code.

There are going to be a few different types of loops that you are able to work with. The first kind is going to be the while loop. This is the one that a programmer would go with for their code when they already know how many times before they start. The code should go through and cycle with the loop. You may use this when you would like the code to count from one to ten because you know exactly when the loop needs to stop. A good example of how the code looks to make the loop show up would be the following:

#calculation of simple interest. Ask the user to input the principal, rate of interest, number of years.

```
counter = 1

while(counter <= 3):

principal = int(input("Enter the principal amount:"))

numberofyeras = int(input("Enter the number of years:"))

rateofinterest = float(input("Enter the rate of interest:"))

simpleinterest = principal * numberofyears * rateofinterest/100

print("Simple interest = %.2f" %simpleinterest)

#increase the counter by 1

counter = counter + 1

print("You have calculated simple interest for 3 time!")
```

Now that we have a good idea of how the while loop works, we need to take a look at the **for loop**. With this one, you let the loop go as many times as it needs until the input is done. This may be one time or it could be ten times. When you work with these for loops, they will not be the one who provides the code with the information to get the loop to start. Instead, this loop is going to complete an iteration in the order that you added it into the code and places it on the screen. There isn't really a need for the user to do this because the loop will just go through all of the iterations that you set up. The code example that you can use to see how this works includes:

Measure some strings:

```
words = ['apple', 'mango', 'banana', 'orange']

for w in words:

print(w, len(w))
```

And finally, we are going to take a look at what is known as a nested loop. This one is going to work a bit differently than the other two in that it is going to have one loop that runs inside of another loop, and it is not done until both of these have reached the end. A good example of when you would want to use this kind of loop would be with a multiplication chart. You do not want to go through the code and write out one times one, and all the way up to ten times ten in order to create the code. A nested loop can take all of it down to just a few lines of code and still make the whole chart. What this would look like is the following:

#write a multiplication table from 1 to 10

```
For x in xrange(1, 11):

For y in xrange(1, 11):

Print '%d = %d' % (x, y, x*x)
```

When you got the output of this program, it is going to look similar to this:

1*1 = 1

1*2 = 2

1*3 = 3

1*4 = 4

All the way up to 1*10 = 10

Then, it would move on to do the table by twos such as this:

2*1 =2

2*2 = 4

And so on until you end up with 10*10 = 100 as your final spot in the sequence.

There is so much that you are able to do when you choose to write out codes in the Python language. This is definitely a language that takes some time to learn and you may have to experiment with some of the codes that come up to make sure that you are using them the proper way. But as it all comes together and you start to put some of these different parts together to form your own code, it will quickly make sense and you will be amazed at all of the things that you are able to do with the Python code.

Chapter 6: Methods and manipulating the ndarray in NumPy

There are several methods and functions available to manipulate ndarrays with the NumPy library. In this section, we will go through the basic methods and functions available and that are crucial to know for data analysis and statistical analysis. This section is presented as questions that we will reply to by presenting the NumPy function to manipulate the arrays with examples of applications.

How to create an empty array or initialized array with 0 or 1 or from a range of values?

To create an empty array function *empty()* can be used. This function will return an array with random values. Input arguments to this function are the shape and the type of data to be storedin the array object. For instance, we can create an array of 6 integer elements with shape (3,2) as follows:

>>> my_array = np.empty([2,3],dtype = int)

>>> print(' My array is:', my_array)

My array is: [[-1018676784 465 0] [0 1 0]]

Note that the values in the array are random because with did not specify the values to be stored in the array.

We can create an array where all values are zeros by using the *zeros()* function. This function takes as input arguments the same input arguments as the *empty()* function, the shape and the type of data. By default, float is assigned as the type of data. So, if type of data is not specified this function will create an array of floats. For instance, we can create an array of size (3,2) as follows:

>>> my_array = np.zeros([2,3])

>>> print(' My array is:', my_array)

My array is: [[0. 0. 0.] [0. 0. 0.]]

Now if we specify the type that we want an array of integers, we get the following result:

>>> my_array = np.zeros([2,3], dtype=np.int)

>>> print(' My array is:', my_array)

My array is: [[0 0 0] [0 0 0]]

As we created an array filled with 0, we can create an array formed with 1 for all items by using the function *ones()*. Like the function's *zeros()* and *empty()*, the *ones()* function takes as input the shape and type of the data where by default the dtype is float. For example:

>>> my_array = np.ones([2,3], dtype=np.int)

>>> print(' My array is:', my_array)

My array is: [[1 1 1] [1 1 1]]

To create an array from a range a value, we use the function arrange(). This function takes as input arguments the first start value, the end value, the step and type of data. For instance, if an array to be created with values from 1 to 10 evenly spaced by 1 (i.e. the step is 1) we can do:

>>> my_array = np.arange(1, 10, 1, dtype=int)

>>> print(' My array from 1 to 10 is:', my_array)

My array from 1 to 10 is: [1 2 3 4 5 6 7 8 9]

In fact, by default the step is 1. So, the array we created above we can created by simply typing:

>>> my_array = np.arange(10)

>>> print(' My array from 1 to 10 is:', my_array)

My array from 1 to 10 is: [0 1 2 3 4 5 6 7 8 9]

Note that, if we don't specify each argument or if we simply pass to the function one argument, this argument is considered as the end value. The function will create an array using the default values which 0 for the start value and 1 for the step.

How to access data of a ndarray in NumPy?

The ndarrays in NumPy can be accessed like the list objects of Python. We can access an item by its position. Remember that the indexing in Python start with 0. For instance, we can get the first item of a random empty array like follows:

>>> my_array = np.empty(5)

>>> print(' My array is:', my_array)

My array is: [9.88332530e-312 2.20687562e-312 2.37663529e-312 7.56602522e-307 1.33508845e-306]

>>> print(' The first item in my array is:', my_array[0])

The first item in my array is: 9.88332530193e-312

We can select few items of an array by slicing. In other words, we can select items that in a range of positions. For instance, we can select the first two rows of an array like follows:

>>> my_A = np.array([[70,90],[100,70],[900,200]])

>>> a = my_A[0:2,]

>>> print(' The first 2 rows are:', a)

The first 2 rows are: [[70 90] [100 70]]

Note that Python does nit include the last index in the output of the slicing. Another way to access the first 2 rows and 2 columns is using the following indexing:

>>> my_A = np.array([[70,90],[100,70],[900,200]])

```
>>> a = my_A[:2,:2]

>>> print(' The result is :', a)

The result is: [[70 90] [100 70]]
```

We can get the items of the first column only by using the following indexing:

```
>>> my_A = np.array([[70,90],[100,70],[900,200]])

>>> a = my_array[:,:1]

>>> print(' Rows of the first columns  are:', a)

Rows of the first columns are: [[70] [100] [900]]
```

The same concept of slicing can be applied to select the elements of a row:

```
>>> my_A = np.array([[70,90],[100,70],[900,200]])

>>> a = my_A[:1,:]

>>> print(' Columns of the first row are:', a)

Columns of the first row are: [[70 90]]
```

How to detect Nan values and Inf values in ndarray in NumPy?

It is very important to detect and handle missing values in data analysis as well as when computing statistics of values in arrays. In general, the missing values should be analyzed and removed before starting a statistical analysis of data. In NumPy, we can detect missing values (i.e. NaN values) or infinite number (i.e. inf) using the functions *numpy.nan()* and *numpy.inf()*. For example, let's create an array and insert a nan value:

```
>>> Y = np.empty(3)

>>> Y[0] = 4
```

```
>>> Y[1] = 2

>>> Y[2] = np.nan

>>> print(' Array is: ', Y)

Array is: [ 4. 2. nan]
```

Now, we can check which items are missing values:

```
>>> print(' Which are nan values:', np.isnan(Y))

Which are nan values: [False False True]
```

The function *numpy.isnan()* outputs a Boolean value. If the item of the array is a missing value it outputs True and False otherwise.

The *numpy.isinf()* as the *isnan()* function outputs a Boolean value. If the item of the array is an infinite value it outputs True and False otherwise. For example, Let's create an array like we did in the previous example:

```
>>> Y = np.empty(3)

>>> Y[0] = 4

>>> Y[1] = 2

>>> Y[2] = np.nan

>>> print(' Array is: ', Y)

Array is: [ 4. 2. inf]

>>> print(' Which are inf values:', np.isinf(Y))

Which are inf values: [False False True]
```

If we want to replace the missing values or the infinite values by specific value, we can change those values by accessing to the position of the missing or infinite values. Let's for example create two arrays where one has a nan value and the other inf value:

```
>>> Y = np.empty(3)

>>> Y[0] = 4

>>> Y[1] = 2

>>> Y[2] = np.nan

>>> print(' Array is : ', Y)
```

Array is : [4. 2. nan]

```
>>> Z = np.empty(3)

>>> Z[0] = 1

>>> Z[1] = 3

>>> Z[2] = np.inf

>>> print(' Array is : ', Z)
```

Array is : [1. 3. inf]

Now we will assign the value -9999 to the missing value and the infinite value:

```
>>> i = np.isnan(Y)

>>> j = np.isinf(Z)

>>> Y[i] = -9999

>>> Z[j] = -9999

>>> print(' My new array Y is:', Y)

>>> print(' My new array Z is:', Z)
```

My new array Y is: [4.0 2.0 -9999]

My new array Z is: [1.0 3.0 -9999]

How to compute basics statistics of an array?

The NumPy library offers several functions to compute the basic statistic of an array that we are going through in this sib-section. The maximum or the minimum values of an array can be computed by calling the functions *max()* and *min()*. These functions are also available in Python. However, in NumPy they have several utilizations that we are going to learn here. Let's first apply the basic functions:

```
>>> Y = np.empty(5,dtype=int)

    >>> print(' My array is:', Y)

    My array is: [1576669984 32765 1576665760 32765 131075]

    >>> print(' The maximum is:', max(Y))

    The maximum is: 1576669984

    >>> print(' The minimum is:', min(Y))

    The minimum is: 32765

    >>> print(' The NumPy max is:', np.max(Y))

    The NumPy max is: 1576669984

    >>> print(' The NumPy minimum is:', np.min(Y))

    The NumPy minimum is: 32765
```

The strength of the NumPy functions is that is allows to compute the maximum and the minimum along the multi-dimensional arrays unlike the functions of Python. To get the idea behind these functions let's create a multi-dimensional array as follows:

```
    >>> my_2dA = np.array( [[90,80,70], [40,70,90]])

    >>> print(' The 2D array is:', my_2dA)
```

My 2D array is: [[90 80 70] [40 70 50]]

Now we can compute the minimum and the maximum along the first dimension of our the 2D array with function *amin()* and *amax()* as follows:

>>> print(' The maximum of rows is', np.amax(my_2dA,0))

The maximum of rows is [90 80 70]

>>> print(' The minimum of rows is', np.amin(my_2dA,0))

The minimum along the first dimension i.e. of rows is [40 70 50]

>>> print(' The maximum of columns is', np.amax(my_2dA,1))

The maximum columns are [90 90]

>>> print(' The minimum of columns is', np.amin(my_2dA,1))

The minimum of columns is [70 50]

Another function that is useful in NumPy is the ptp() function which returns the range values of the elements of an array. In other words, it returns the maximum and the minimum range of values of an array along a certain dimension. Let's apply this function to our 2D array:

>>> my_2dA = np.array([[90,80,70], [40,70,90]])

>>> print(' The 2D array is:', my_2dA)

>>> print(' Applying the ptp function gives:', np.ptp(my_2dA))

My 2D array is: [[90 80 70] [40 70 50]]

Applying the ptp function gives: 70

>>> print(' Applying the ptp function gives along the 1st dim', np.ptp(my_2dA,0))

Applying the ptp function gives along the 1st dim [70 70 70]

>>> print(' Applying the ptp function gives along the 2nd dim', np.ptp(my_2darray,1))

Applying the ptp function gives along the 2nd dim [80 80]

We can compute a percentile of the values in array by using the *percentile()* function. The percentile in statistics is the value that divides the range of value into blocks of a certain percentage of number of items of a set of values. For instance, the percentile 50 which is the median is the value that divides a set of values into 2 equal blocks. In other words, 50% of the data are below the median value and 50 % are above the median value. The *percentile()* function takes as input an array and the percentile to compute that is given as a value between 1 and 100 and the axis or dimension along which the function will compute the percentile. Now let's apply this function on our 2D array:

>>> my_2dA = np.array([[90,80,70], [40,70,90]])

>>> print(' The 2D array is:', my_2dA)

My 2D array is: [[90 80 70] [40 70 50]]

>>> print(' The percentile 50 along the 1st axis is:', np.percentile(my_2dA,0))

The percentile 50 along the 1st axis is: 70

>>> print(' The percentile 50 along the 1st axis is:', np.percentile(my_2dA,1))

The percentile 50 along the 1st axis is: 50

If you are interested in computing the median, the function *median()* can be called as presented below:

>>> print(' The median along the 1st axis is:', np.percentile(my_2dA,0))

The median along the 1st axis is: 70

The mean and the weighted average of an array can be computed by calling the *mean()* and the *average()* functions. The difference between these two functions is that the first one compute the arithmetic mean which is the ratio of the sum of the values by total number of the array items while the second weighted sum compute the ratio of weighted sum of item values by their total number. Two input arguments as arrays should be supplied to the *average()* function with the second one is the weight assigned to each item in the first array. If the second input argument i.e. weight array is not passed to this function it computes the arithmetic mean like the *mean()* function.

>>> My_array = np.empty(5,dtype=np.int8)

>>> print(' My array is:', My_array)

My array is: [1 2 34 5 6]

>>> print(' The mean of my array is:', np.mean(My_array))

The mean of my array is: 9.6

>>> print(' The average of my array is:', np.average(My_array))

The average of my array is: 9.6

See in the example above the *mean()* function and the *average()* function provide the same result because we did not supply the average function with a weight array. So, if we have a weight that represent the importance of every element of My_array we can compute the weighted average as follows:

>>> weights = np.array([2,4,1,2,3])

>>> print(' My weights are:', weights)

My weights are: [2 4 1 2 3]

>>> print(' The weighted average of my array is:', np.average(My_array, weights=weights))

The weighted average of my array is: 6.0

The average function can also return the sum of the weights if we supply a third input argument which a Boolean named returned. If this argument is set to True it will return the sum. By default, this argument is set False so it does not return the sum of weights by default.

>>> print(' The weighted average and sum of weights of my array is:', np.average(My_array,weights=weights, returned='True'))

The weighted average of my array is: (6.0, 12.0)

To compute the standard deviation and the variance of an array we can call the two following functions *std()* and *var()*. If we apply these functions on the previous array we created My_array, we get:

>>> print(' My array is:', My_array)

>>> print (' The standard deviation of my array is:', np.std(My_array))

>>> print (' The variance of my array is:', np.var(My_array))

My array is: [1 2 34 5 6]

The standard deviation of my array is: 12.338

The variance of my array is: 152.239

How to sort and search for specific value in ndarray in NumPy?

In order to sort an array in NumPy we use the function *sort()*. This function sorts the items of multi-dimensional array according to the specified axis. By default, the sort function will sort the values according to the first axis if no axis is specified. Let's sort the array we worked with before:

>>> print(' My array is:', My_array)

>>> print(' My sorted array is:', np.sort(My_array))

My array is: [1 2 34 5 6]

My sorted array is: [1 2 5 6 34]

If we have a multi-dimensional array like in the example below, we can specify an axis along which to sort the data as follows:

>>> my_2darray = np.array([[1000,20,300],[400,50,600]])

>>> print(' My 2D array is:', my_2darray)

>>> print(' My 2D array sorted along axis 1 is:', np.sort(my_2darray,0))

>>> print(' My 2D array sorted along axis 2 is:', np.sort(my_2darray,1))

My 2D array is: [[1000 20 300] [400 50 600]]

My 2D array sorted along axis 1 is:

[[400 20 300] [1000 50 600]]

My 2D array sorted along axis 2 is:

[[20 300 1000] [50 400 600]]

We have learnt before in this section how to get the minimum and maximum values of an array, but we did not learn how to get the position of the minimum and the maximum values. The functions *argmax()* and *argmin()* provide to the position of the min and max values.

>>> my_2darray = np.array([[1000,20,300],[400,50,600]])

>>> print(' My 2D array is:', my_2darray)

>>> print(' The indices of min values of first axis 1 are:', np.argmin(my_2darray,0))

>>> print('The indices of min values of second axis are:', np.argmin(my_2darray,1))

My 2D array is: [[1000 20 300] [400 50 600]]

The indices of min values of first axis are: [1 0 0]

The indices of the min values of second axis are: [1 1]

>>> print(' The indices of max values of first axis are:', np.argmax(my_2darray,0))

>>> print(' The indices of max values of second axis are:', np.argmax(my_2darray,1))

The indices of the max values of first axis are: [0 1 1]

The indices of the max values of second axis 2 are: [0 2]

Now we will see how to search for specific values in an array or items using conditions. The most common value we can search for is the non null values in array i.e. items that are not equal to 0. To do so NumPy offers the function *nonzero()*. This function returns the positions of the items that are not equal to 0. For example:

>>> my_2darray = np.array([[1000,0,300],[400,50,0]])

>>> print(' My 2D array is:', my_2darray)

>>> print(' Position of non-zero items:', np.nonzero(my_2darray))

My 2D array is: [[1000 200 300] [400 50 0]]

Position of non-zero items: (array([0, 0, 0, 1], dtype=int64), array([0, 2, 0, 1], dtype=int64))

If we you are searching for items in array that are greater or lower than a certain value, the function *where()* can be used. For instance, let's get the position of all items that are greater than 50 in our 2D array:

>>> my_2darray = np.array([[9, 90,300],[400,50,0]])

>>> print(' My 2D array is:', my_2darray)

>>> i = np.where(my_2darray>50)

>>> print(' The position of the items > 50 are: ', i)

My 2D array is: [[9 90 300] [400 50 0]]

The position of the items > 50 are: (array([0, 1, 1], dtype=int64), array([1, 2, 1], dtype=int64))

Now we can access the items with values superior to 50 through the indices stored in the variable i and change those values to 1 for example:

>>> my_2darray[i]=1

>>> print(' My new array is:', my_2darray)

My new array is: [[1 0 1] [1 50 0]]

Overall, we can search for items that satisfy a condition by using the function *extract()*. To use this function, the condition must be defined first. Let's search for the items that has a value superior to 50 in our 2D array but with extract function.

>>> my_2darray = np.array([[1000,0,300],[400,50,0]])

>>> print(' My 2D array is:', my_2darray)

My 2D array is: [[1000 0 300] [400 50 0]]

We define our condition my_2darray > 50:

>>> cond = my_2darray>50

```
>>> i= np.extract(cond,my_2darray)

>>> print(' Items with values >50 are:', i)

Items with values >50 are: [1000 300 400]
```

Note that extract function does not return the positions but the items themselves that satisfy the condition.

Chapter 7: Data frames

A Pandas data frame is just an ordered collection of Pandas series with a common/shared index. At its basic form, a data frame looks more like an excel sheet with rows, columns, labels and headers. To create a data frame, the following syntax is used:

pd.DataFrame(data=None, index=None, columns=None, dtype=None, copy=False)

Usually, the data input is an array of values (of whatever datatype). The index and column parameters are usually lists/vectors of either numeric or string type.

If a Pandas series is passed to a data frame object, the index automatically becomes the columns, and the data points are assigned accordingly.

Example 71: Creating a data frame

In []: df = pd.DataFrame([pool1])   *# passing a series*

df   *# show*

two series

index = 'WWI WWII'.split()

new_df = pd.DataFrame([pool1,pool3],index)
         new_df   *# show*

Output:

USA	Britain	France	Germany	
0	1	2	3	4

	USA	Britain	France	Germany
WWI	1	2	3	4
WWII	5	1	3	4

For the second data frame, the row labels were specified by passing a list of strings ['WWI','WWII'].

> *Tip:* The **.split()** string method is a quick way of creating lists of strings. It works by splitting a string into its component characters, depending on the delimiter passed to the string method.
>
> For example, let us split this email 'pythonguy@gmail.com' into a list containing the username and the domain name.

In []: # Illustrating the split() method

email = 'pythonguy@gmail.com'

string_vec = email.split('@')

string_vec   # show

A = string_vec[0]; B = string_vec[1] # *Extracting values*

print('Username:',A,'\nDomain name:',B)

Out[]: ['pythonguy', 'gmail.com']

   Username: pythonguy

   Domain name: gmail.com

To create a data frame with an array, we can use the following method:

Creating dataframe with an array

```
Array = np.arange(1,21).reshape(5,4)  # numpy array

row_labels = 'A B C D E'.split()

col_labels = 'odd1 even1 odd2 even2'.split()

Arr_df = pd.DataFrame(Array,row_labels,col_labels)

Arr_df
```
Output:

	odd1	even1	odd2	even2
A	1	2	3	4
B	5	6	7	8
C	9	10	11	12
D	13	14	15	16
E	17	18	19	20

Notice how this is not unlike how we create spreadsheets in excel. Try playing around with creating data frames.

Exercise: Create a data frame from a 5 × 4 array of uniformly distributed random values. Include your choice row and column names using the **.split()** method.

> *Hint:* use the rand function to generate your values, and use the reshape method to form an array.

Now that we can conveniently create Data frames, we are going to learn how to index and grab elements off them.

> *Tip:* Things to note about data frames.

- *They are a collection of series (more like a list with Pandas series as its elements).*
- *They are similar to numpy arrays i.e. they are more like n $\times$ m dimensional matrices, where 'n' are the rows and 'm' are the columns.*

Example 72: Grabbing elements from a data frame.

The easiest elements to grab are the columns. This is because, by default, each column element is a series with the row headers as labels. We can grab them by using a similar method from the series – indexing by name.

In []: # Grab data frame elements

 Arr_df['odd1']   # grabbing first column

Out[]: A   1

 B   5

 C   9

 D   13

 E   17

 Name: odd1, dtype: int32

Pretty easy, right? Notice how the output is like a Pandas series. You can verify this by using the **type(Arr_df['odd1'])** command.

When more than one column is grabbed, however, it returns a data frame (which makes sense, since a data frame is a collection of at least two series). To grab more than one column, pass the column names to the indexing as a list. This is shown in the example code below:

In []:# Grab two columns

 Arr_df[['odd1','even2']] # grabbing first and last columns
Output:

	odd1	even2
A	1	4
B	5	8
C	9	12
D	13	16
E	17	20

To select a specific element, use the double square brackets indexing notation we learned under array indexing. For example, let us select the value 15 from Arr_df.

In []: Arr_df['odd2']['D']
     Out[]: 15

You may decide to break the steps into two, if it makes it easier. This method is however preferred as it saves memory from variable allocation. To explain, let us break it down into two steps.

In []: x = Arr_df['odd2']

x

Out[]: A   3

B   7

C   11

D   15

E   19

Name: odd2, dtype: int32

See that the first operation returns a series containing the element '15'. This series can now be indexed to grab 15 using the label 'D'.

In []: x['D']

　　　　Out[]: 15

While this approach works, and is preferred by beginners, a better approach is to get comfortable with the first method to save coding time and resources.

To grab rows, a different indexing method is used.

You can use either **data_frame_name.loc['row_name']** or **data_frame_name.iloc['row_index']**.

Let us grab the row E from **Arr_df**.

In []: print("using .loc['E']")

　　Arr_df.loc['E']

　　print('\nusing .iloc[4]')

　　Arr_df.iloc[4]

　　　using .loc['E']

Out[]:

　　odd1　　17

　　even1　　18

　　odd2　　19

　　even2　　20

　　Name: E, dtype: int32

　　　using .iloc[4]

Out[]:

　　odd1　　17

even1   18

odd2   19

even2   20

Name: E, dtype: int32

See, the same result!

You can also use the row indexing method to select single items.

In []: Arr_df.loc['E']['even2']

  # or

  Arr_df.iloc[4]['even2']

Out[]: 20

Out[]: 20

Moving on, we will try to create new columns in a data frame, and also delete a column.

In []: # Let us add two sum columns to Arr_df

Arr_df['Odd sum'] = Arr_df['odd1']+Arr_df['odd2']

Arr_df['Even sum'] = Arr_df['even1']+Arr_df['even2']

Arr_df

Output:

	odd1	even1	odd2	even2	Odd sum	Even sum
A	1	2	3	4	4	6
B	5	6	7	8	12	14
C	9	10	11	12	20	22
D	13	14	15	16	28	30
E	17	18	19	20	36	38

Notice how the new columns are declared. Also, arithmetic operations are possible with each element in the data frame, just like we did with the series.

Exercise: Add an extra column to this data frame. Call it Total Sum, and it should be the addition of Odd sum and Even sum.

To remove a column from a data frame, we use the **data_frame_name.drop()** method.

Let us remove the insert a new column and then remove it using the **.drop()** method.

In []: Arr_df['disposable'] = np.zeros(5)   *# new column*
                    Arr_df   *#show*

Output:

	odd1	even1	odd2	even2	Odd sum	Even sum	disposable
A	1	2	3	4	4	6	0.0
B	5	6	7	8	12	14	0.0
C	9	10	11	12	20	22	0.0
D	13	14	15	16	28	30	0.0
E	17	18	19	20	36	38	0.0

To remove the unwanted column:

In []: # to remove

Arr_df.drop('disposable',axis=1,inplace=True)

Arr_df

Output:

	odd1	even1	odd2	even2	Odd sum	Even sum
A	1	2	3	4	4	6
B	5	6	7	8	12	14
C	9	10	11	12	20	22
D	13	14	15	16	28	30
E	17	18	19	20	36	38

Notice the 'axis=1' and 'inplace = True' arguments. These are parameters that specify the location to perform the drop i.e. axis (axis = 0 specifies row operation), and intention to broadcast the drop to the original data frame, respectively. If 'inplace= False', the data frame will still contain the dropped column.

Tip: The 'inplace = False' method is used for assigning an array to another variable without including certain columns.

Conditional selection

Similar to how we conditional selection works with NumPy arrays, we can select elements from a data frame that satisfy a Boolean criterion.

You are expected to be familiar with this method, hence, it will be done in one step.

Example 72: Let us grab sections of the data frame 'Arr_df' where the value is > 5.

In []: # Grab elements greater than five
          Arr_df[Arr_df>5]

Output:

	odd1	even1	odd2	even2	Odd sum	Even sum
A	NaN	NaN	NaN	NaN	NaN	6
B	NaN	6.0	7.0	8.0	12.0	14
C	9.0	10.0	11.0	12.0	20.0	22
D	13.0	14.0	15.0	16.0	28.0	30
E	17.0	18.0	19.0	20.0	36.0	38

Notice how the instances of values less than 5 are represented with a 'NaN'.

Another way to use this conditional formatting is to format based on column specifications.

You could remove entire rows of data, by specifying a Boolean condition based off a single column. Assuming we want to return the Arr_df data frame without the row 'C'. We can specify a condition to return values where the elements of column 'odd1' are not equal to '9' (since row C contains 9 under column 'odd1').

In []: # removing row C through the first column
          Arr_df[Arr_df['odd1']!= 9]

Output:

	odd1	even1	odd2	even2	Odd sum	Even sum
A	1	2	3	4	4	6
B	5	6	7	8	12	14

D	13	14	15	16	28	30
E	17	18	19	20	36	38

Notice that row 'C' has been filtered out. This can be achieved through a smart conditional statement through any of the columns.

In []: # does the same thing : remove row 'C'

    # Arr_df[Arr_df['even2']!= 12]

In[]: # Let us remove rows D and E through 'even2'
                     Arr_df[Arr_df['even2']<= 12]

Output

	odd1	even1	odd2	even2	Odd sum	Even sum
A	1	2	3	4	4	6
B	5	6	7	8	12	14
C	9	10	11	12	20	22

Exercise: Remove rows C, D, E via the 'Even sum' column. Also, try out other such operations as you may prefer.

To combine conditional selection statements, we can use the 'logical and, i.e. &', and the 'logical or, i.e. |' for nesting multiple conditions. The regular 'and' and 'or' operators would not work in this case as they are used for comparing single elements. Here, we will be comparing a series of elements that evaluates to true or false, and those generic operators find such operations ambiguous.

Example 73: Let us select elements that meet the criteria of being greater than 1 in the first column, and less than 22 in the last column. Remember, the 'and statement' only evaluates to true if both conditions are true.

In []:Arr_df[(Arr_df['odd1']>1) & (Arr_df['Even sum']<22)]
Output:

odd1	even1	odd2	even2	Odd sum	Even sum
5	6	7	8		

Only the elements in Row 'B' meet this criterion, and were returned in the data frame.

This approach can be expounded upon to create even more powerful data frame filters.

Missing Data

There are instances when the data being imported or generated into pandas is incomplete or have missing data points. In such a case, the likely solution is to remove such values from the dataset, or to fill in new values based on some statistical extrapolation techniques. While we would not be fully exploring statistical measures of extrapolation (you can read up on that from any good statistics textbook), we would be considering the use of the **.dropna()** and **.fillna()** methods for removing and filling up missing data points respectively.

To illustrate this, we will create a data frame – to represent imported data with missing values, and then use these two data preparation methods on it.

Example 73: Another way to create a data frame is by using a dictionary. Remember, a python dictionary is somehow similar to a Pandas series in that they have key-value pairs, just as Pandas series are label-value pairs (although this is a simplistic comparison for the sake of conceptualization).

In []:# First, our dictionary

dico = {'X':[1,2,np.nan],'Y':[4,np.nan,np.nan],'Z':[7,8,9]}

dico #show

passing the dictionary to a dataframe

row_labels = 'A B C'.split()

df = pd.DataFrame(dico,row_labels)

df #show

Output:

{'X': [1, 2, nan], 'Y': [4, nan, nan], 'Z': [7, 8, 9]}

	X	Y	Z
A	1.0	4.0	7
B	2.0	NaN	8
C	NaN	NaN	9

Now, let us start off with the **.dropna()** method. This removes any 'null' or 'nan' values in the data frame it's called off, either column-wise or row-wise, depending on the axis specification and other arguments passed to the method. It has the following default syntax:

```
df.dropna(axis=0, how='any', thresh=None, subset=None, inplace=False)
```

The 'df' above is the data frame name. The default axis is set to zero, which represent row-wise operation. Hence, at default, the method will remove any row containing 'nan' values.

Let us see what happens when we call this method for our data frame.

In []: # this removes 'nan' row-wise
            df.dropna()

Output:	X	Y	Z
A	1.0	4.0	7

Notice that rows B and C contain at least a 'nan' value. Hence, they were removed.

Let us try a column-wise operation by specifying the axis=1.

In []: # this removes 'nan' column-wise
            df.dropna(axis=1)

Output:

	Z
A	7
B	8
C	9

As expected, only the column 'Z' was returned.

Now, in case we want to set a condition for a minimum number of 'non-nan' values/ actual data points required to make the cut (or escape the cut, depending on your perspective), we can use the 'thresh' (short for threshold) parameter to specify this.

Say, we want to remove 'nan' row-wise, but we only want to remove instances where the row had more than one actual data point value. We can set the threshold to 2 as illustrated in the following code:

In []: # drop rows with less than 2 actual values
            df.dropna(thresh = 2)

Output:

	X	Y	Z
A	1.0	4.0	7
B	2.0	NaN	8

Notice how we have filtered out row C, since it contains only one actual value '9'.

Exercise: Filter out columns in the data frame 'df' containing less than 2 actual data points

Next, let us use the **.fillna()** method to replace the missing values with our extrapolations.

This method has the following syntax:

df.fillna(value=None, method=None, axis=None, inplace=False,
            limit=None, downcast=None, **kwargs)

    Tip: Reminder, you can always use **shift + tab** to check the

        documentation of methods and functions to know their syntax.

Let us go ahead and replace our 'NaN' values with an 'x' marker. We can specify the 'X' as a string, and pass it into the 'value' parameter in **.fillna()**.

In []: # filling up NaNs
    df.fillna('X')

Output:	X	Y	Z
A	1	4	7
B	2	X	8
C	X	X	9

While marking missing data with an 'X' is fun, it is sometimes more intuitive (for lack of a better statistical approach), to use the mean of the affected column as a replacement for the missing elements.

Example 74: Filling up missing data.

Let us first use the mean method to fill up column 'X', then based off that simple step, we will use a for loop to automatically fill up missing data in the data frame.

In []: # Replacing missing values with mean in column 'X'

df['X'].fillna(value = df['X'].mean())

Out[]: A   1.0

B   2.0

C   1.5

Name: X, dtype: float64

Notice that the value of the third element in column 'X' has changed to 1.5. This is the mean of that column. The one line code that accomplished this could have been broken down into multiple line for better understanding. This is shown below:

In []:# variables
    xcol_var = df['X']

```
xcol_mean = xcol_var.mean()  # or use mean(xcol_var)
# instruction
xcol_var.fillna(value = xcol_mean)
Out[]: A    1.0
B    2.0
C    1.5
```

Name: X, dtype: float64

Same results, but more coding and more memory use via variable allocation.

Now, let us automate the entire process.

```
In []: for i in 'X Y Z'.split():          # loop

    df[i].fillna(value = df[i].mean(),inplace=True)
                df          # show
```

Output:

	X	Y	Z
A	1.0	4.0	7
B	2.0	NaN	8
C	NaN	NaN	9

	X	Y	Z
A	1.0	4.0	7
B	2.0	4.0	8
C	1.5	4.0	9

New data frame   Old data frame

While the output only displays the data frame on the left, the original data frame is put here for comparison. Notice the new values replacing the NaNs. For the column 'Y', the mean is 4.0, since that is the only value present.

This is a small operation that can be scaled for preparing and formatting larger datasets in Pandas.

> *Tip:* The other arguments of the **.fillna()** method can be
>
> explored, including the fill methods: for example, forward-fill -
>
> which fills the missing value with the previous row/column
>
> value based on the value of the limit parameter i.e. if limit = 1, it
>
> fills the next 1 row/column with the previous row/column
>
> value; also, the back-fill - which does the same as forward-fill,
>
> but backwards.

Group-By

This Pandas method, as the name suggests, allows the grouping of related data to perform combined/aggregate operations on them.

Example 75: Creating a data frame of XYZ store sales.

In []: # Company XYZ sales information

    # Dictionary containing needed data

data = {'Sales Person':'Sam Charlie Amy Vanessa Carl Sarah'.split(),

    'Product':'Hp Hp Apple Apple Dell Dell'.split(),

    'Sales':[200,120,340,124,243,350]}

print('XYZ sales information\n_____') # *print info.*

```
serial = list(range(1,7))      # row names from 1-6

df = pd.DataFrame(data,serial)   # build data frame

df
```

Output:

Chapter 8: IPython and Jupyter Notebooks

IPython and Jupyter Notebooks are two great tools capable of interactive computing and rich media output. Combined they offer a great skillset for a Data Scientist. Let's dive in details about each of these.

IPython

IPython also known as Interactive Python is a capable toolkit that allow you to experience Python interactively. It has two main components: an interactive Python Shell interface, and Jupyter kernels.

These components have many features, such as:

Persistent input history

Caching of outputs

Code completition

Support for 'magic' commands

Highly customizable settings

Syntax highlighting

Session logging

Access to system Shell

Support to python's debugger and profiler

Now, let's dive into each of these components and see how these features come to life.

Installing IPython

Using *pip*, run the command:

With conda, just type:

IPython Shell

The objective of this Shell is to provide a superior experience than the default Python REPL.

To run the IPython Shell you just need to call the command bellow on your system console.

§ Interface

At first glance, the IPython Shell looks like a normal boring Shell, some initial version information and some user tips. However, it has great features that make it shine.

§ Help

You can type "?" after an accessible object at any time you want more details about it.

§ Code Completition

You can press "TAB" key at any time to trigger the code completition.

§ Syntax Highlight

The code is automatically highlighted depending on the variables and keywords you are using.

§ Run External Commands

External commands can be run directly using "!" in the beginning of the input.

§ Magic Commands

Magic commands add incredible capabilities to IPython. Some commands are shown bellow:

%time – Shows the time to execute the command.

%timeit – Shows the mean and standard deviation of the time to execute the command.

%pdb – Run the code in debug mode, creating breakpoints on uncaught exceptions.

%matplotlib – This command arranges all the setup needed to IPython work correctly with matplotlib, this way IPython can display plots that are outputs of running code in new windows.

There are multiple magic commands that be used on IPython Shell, for a full list of the built-in commands check this LINK or type "%lsmagic".

Jupyter Notebooks

The Jupyter Notebook is an incredible browser-based tool used to combine code, text, mathematics, graphs, and media in general. It expands the usual console approach bringing a web-based application capable of developing, executing and documenting the code.

To run a Jupyter Notebook you just need to call the command bellow on your system console.

After running this command, a new window will pop up on your default browser with an interface, let's explore it.

§ Dashboard

This is the Jupyter notebook Dashboard, it is where locally stored notebooks are displayed. It works like a file explorer. As you can see, there is no notebooks, lets change it by creating a new one by clicking on New->Notebook: Python 3 as shown.

§ Notebook Editor

Now you are ready to edit your own notebook, but first let's be familiar with the interface items listed above.

1.

This is the notebook Cell, it is the simpler component of a notebook.

2.

This drop-down menu alternates the kind of the selected cell. Each cell can have one of three types: Code, Markdown and Raw.

3.

This is the button that adds more cells to the notebook.

4.

This button executes the current cells and selects the next one.

Ok, after this brief description of the main interface elements, we can start creating our notebook.

§ Cell Basics

Any of the tree types of cell have two possible modes, *Command* and *Edit*.

Command Mode: The cell left edge is blue and typing will send commands to the notebook. If in edit mode, you can change to command mode with the "ESC" key.

Edit Mode: The cell left edge is green and there is a small grey pencil in the top right corner ( ), typing in this mode will edit the content of the cell. This mode can be achieved double clicking a markdown cell or single clicking a code/raw cell. If in command mode, you can change to edit mode with the "Enter" key.

Running: Any cell can be executed using the interface button or the shortcuts:

"Ctrl+Enter": Run the current cell.

"Shift+Enter": Run the current cell and move to the next one.

Code Cells: Code cells can execute Python code. Any code not assigned to a variable will be shown as the output of the cell. Code cells have a "In []" on its left, indicating that it is an input cell and the number inside the bracket reveals the order of execution.

Markdown Cells: This is how text can be added to the notebook. Markdown is a popular markup language that adds formatting to the text when rendered. The markdown language is only rendered after the cell execution, but in edit mode the cell highlights the modifications that will be performed during rendering.

§ Rich Media Output

One of the greatest advantages of Jupyter Notebooks are their capabilities of representing media. Code cells have built-in integration with matplotlib graphs, and many other kinds of media.

Matplotlib Plots: Any matplotlib plot shown during a cell execution will be displayed in the cell output.

Audio Clips: Audio media can be displayed.

Video Clips: Video media can also be easily shown.

Tables: Tabular data visualization.

Chapter 9: Numpy for Numerical Data Processing

In this chapter, we will explore a fundamental package for data analysis: Numpy. It has powerful multi-dimensional array capabilities with fast high-level mathematical operations and handy functions. When explaining concepts in multi-dimensional arrays, we will focus first explain in one dimension to easily create the generalization for the concept.

Numpy

Numpy is one of the most famous and widely used Python packages for efficient data processing. Its main object is the multi-dimensional array: *ndarray*. Some algorithms can have considerable performance increase using the array class offered by the numpy library. Additionally, the SCIPY ecosystem of software are built on top of this to provide various scientific and engineering methods.

Installing IPython

Using pip, run the command:

With conda, just type:

Generally, numpy is imported using the short *np* as alias:

Object ndarray

This is the main object implemented by the numpy package. Simply put, it is a multidimensional ordered container object. However, differently of

Python's built-in list numpy arrays are homogeneous, i.e. all elements should be the same type.

Creating and Modifying Arrays

An array can be created using any array-like ordered objects in Python, such as lists or tuples. In order to create an array the function *np.array()* is called with the list object. The type can be inferred from the data or given as an argument.

§ One-dimensional Arrays

The type be given to the *np.array()* command with the *dtype* keyword. Additionally, the type and dimension of the created array can be checked using the *dtype* and *ndim* class attributes, respectively.

OBS1.: From now on, we will assume that numpy is imported as the alias np in all the IPYTHON SHELL examples.

OBS2.: Notice that a single value can be considered an array with dimension 0.

§ Multi-dimensional Arrays

Nested and array-like objects are used to construct the dimensions of the array. You can think of multidimensional array as a set of the arrays in previous dimension. For instance, we have seen that 0-dimensinal array corresponds to a single value, then a 1-dimensional array is a set of 0-dimensional arrays. And a 2-dimensional array is a set of 1-dimensional arrays and so on. This concept is illustrated in the table below.

The same logic follows for more than 3 dimensions, you can think a 4-dimensional array as a of collection of Cubes arrays. However, beyond 3 dimensions it is not easily illustratable and intuitive. The attributes *shape* and *size* are useful attributes for multi-dimensional arrays. The first returns the size of the array in each dimension, the second returns the total number of elements present in the array.

OBS.: As shown in array c, be careful with the number of values in each dimension of the array. They should be consistent along the definition, otherwise the dimension will be ignored, and you create an array of lists.

§ Creating Filled Arrays

In general, it is common to create arrays filled with a constant value or with a range of values. For that there are 5 useful functions in Numpy: np.zeros(), np.ones(), np.full(), np.linspace(), np.arange(). The examples illustrate the behavior of the functions.

OBS.: Prefer to use np.linspace() over np.arange() for arrays with float values to have predictable number of values.

§ Reshaping Arrays

Created arrays can be reshape with the *reshape* method. The only restriction is that the new format should have the same number values as the previous. If one dimension is set to -1, the dimension is inferred from the remaining. The method *ravel* returns a flattened view.

§ Appending to Arrays

Differently of lists, numpy arrays have fixed sizes. Therefore, to append a value in the array a new array is created, and the values are copied. This can be done with the *append* function which accepts values or other arrays. For large arrays, this is a costly operation and should be avoided. A good practice is to create the array with extra spaces and fill it.

§ Stacking and Concatenating Arrays

There are several functions that can perform the combinations of arrays, such as *hstack* and *vstack*. These functions are easily understandable when applied to arrays up to 3 dimensions, for more dimensions the general functions *stack* and *concatenate* are more appropriate.

Indexing, Slicing and Iterating

Operation to access values or range of values from an array. As well as iterate over its values.

§ One-dimensional Arrays

The slicing, indexing and iterating with one-dimensional arrays is equivalent to the same operation on normal Python lists. The same logic can be used to change values on the array.

§ Multi-dimensional Arrays

Indexing arrays with multiple dimension are done with a tuple with a value for each dimension. However, if an index value is omitted, it is considered a complete slice, which is equivalent to ":". Additionally, the "..." can be used in the indexes to represent as many as ":" as needed. Iterating on multidimensional array is always performed in the first dimension. Numpy has also the capability to perform each element iteration with the *np.nditer* function, but this function treats the values as read-only by default. In general, it is easier and more intuitive to use the first dimension during iteration over the multidimensional array.

```
>>> mat = np.arange(9).reshape((3,3))
                        # 3x3 Matrix from 0 to 8
>>> mat
array([[0, 1, 2],
       [3, 4, 5],
       [6, 7, 8]])
>>> mat[1, 1]              # Indexing
4
>>> mat[1, :]             # Slicing
array([3, 4, 5])
>>> mat[1]               # Equivalent
array([3, 4, 5])

>>> mat[0, :]
array([6, 7, 8])
>>> mat[0, ...]           # Equivalent
array([6, 7, 8])

>>> for row in mat:       # Iterating on the first dimension
>>>     print(row)
[0 1 2]
[3 4 5]
[6 7 8]
>>> for row in mat:       # Iterating on the first dimension
>>>     print(row)
[0 1 2]
[3 4 5]
[6 7 8]
>>> for v in np.nditer(mat): # Iterating each value
>>>     print(v)
0
1
2
3
4
5
6
7
8
```

§ Boolean Indexing

Numpy array also allow Boolean indexing. True and False means if the value will be returned or not, respectively. You can use boolean indexing to perform filter operations on arrays, such as get values above or below a given threshold. Additionally, multiple conditions can be performed at the same time and more advanced filters created with this type of indexing. This can simply be done by using comparison operations between arrays and values. The operators & (and), |(or) are used to combine multiple conditions between parentheses.

This is the best way to filter specific values in a numpy array.

Operations and Functions

Numpy arrays, support arithmetic operations as expected. Here we will see some caveats of Broadcasting and built-in functions of the arrays.

Basic Operations

Same basic operations present in standard Python are also present in Numpy arrays. In this case, the operation between arrays of same shape results in another array.

Advanced Operations

There is also support for operations and transformations beyond the basics. Some advanced matrix operations are easily usable by functions in the *linalg* name space, attributes and methods of the object. For example, matrix product, determinant, inverse, etc.

Broadcasting

Broadcasting is a great feature that allow great flexibility. Shortly, broadcasting is the ability to perform operation between arrays that do not have exact same size or shape. It is based in two rules:

1.

If an array has fewer dimensions a '1' will prepended to the shape of this array until both arrays have the same dimensions.

2.

Arrays with size 1 in a specific dimension performs as if they had the same dimension of the array with the largest size in that dimension.

Do not worry, these rules are not easily understandable when written but they make perfect sense on examples. Additionally, broadcasting allows vectorized operations with high performance and memory efficiency. The name comes from the fact that the smaller array is 'broadcasted' to fit the dimension of the larger one. Examples and detailed explanations are shown below:

In *Example 1* the first thing that happens is to fit the scalar value in the same dimension as the array a, resulting in an array *np.array([1])*. Then, since this dimension has size 1, it will be broadcasted to fit the size of the larger array, in this case 4. As shown, that is equivalent to the operation execute in the array *c*.

While in *Example 2*, the scalar value is converted to the array *np.array([[-1]])*. After that, the dimensions with size 1 will be extended to fit the larger array, in this case 2 for dimension 0 and 2 for dimension 1. Similarly, the array *c* presents same result.

The *Examples 3* and *4* show similar behavior but with more dimension. First, the dimension is added to the array *b* to have the same dimension of *a*. Then, the array is repeated in this dimension fit the larger array.

Built-in Functions

In addition to operations, arrays have multiple functions to facilitate descriptive statistics calculations. Additionally the namespace random contains functions to create random variable in multiple different types of distributions. Now we will be using the *randn*, which receives the size of the desired array sample from a normal distribution with mean 0 and standard deviation 1.

```
IPYTHON SHELL:
>>> np.random.seed(42)          # Replicability
>>> a = np.random.randn(50)     # 50 values from
                                  normal distribution
>>> a.mean()                    # Mean
-0.28385754369506705
>>> a.std()                     # Standard Deviation
0.8801815954843186
>>> a.max()                     # Max value
1.8522781845089378
>>> a.min()                     # Min value
-1.9596701238797756
>>> a.argmax()                  # Index of max value
22
>>> a.sum()                     # Sum of values
-14.192877184753353

>>> a.reshape((2, 25)).mean(axis=1) # Mean on axis 1
(lines)
array([-0.37612378, -0.19159131])
```

OBS1: The seed function guarantees replicability of the result. Otherwise, the results will change since the values are sampled from a random function.

OBS2: For multidimensional arrays the functions can be applied in a specific dimension, with axis=0 being in the columns and axis=1 the rows. This is shown in the last example.

Chapter 10: Challenges of Categorical Data

Categorical attributes can contain multiple levels, called "high cardinality" (e.g. states, towns or URLs), where most levels appear in a relatively smaller number of instances.

Various ML models are algebraic, such as "regression" and "SVM", which require numerical input. Categories have to be changed first to numbers to use these models before the machine learning algorithm can be applied.

While some machine learning packages or libraries are capable of automatically transforming the categorical data into numeric, depending on the default embedded technique, a variety of machine learning libraries don't support categorical data inputs.

Categorical data for the computer does not translate the context or background, that people can readily associate with and comprehend. For instance, consider a function called "City" with different city names like "New York", "New Jersey", and "New Delhi". People know that "New York" is strongly linked to "New Jersey" being two neighboring states of America, while "New York" and "New Delhi" are very distinct. On the other hand, for the machine, all three cities just denote three distinct levels of the same "City" function. Without specifying adequate context through data for the model, differentiating between extremely distinct levels will be difficult for it.

Encoding Categorical Data

Machine learning models are built on mathematical equations, so it is easy to comprehend that maintaining the categorical data in equations would cause issues since equations are primarily driven by numbers alone. To cross this hurdle, the categorical features can be encoded to numeric quantities.

The encoding techniques below will be described using example of an "airline carrier" column from a make-believe airline database, for ease of understanding. However, it is possible to extend the same techniques to any desired column.

1. Replacing the categorical values

This is a fundamental technique of replacing the categorical data values with required integers. The *"replace()"* function in Pandas, can be used for this technique. Depending on your business requirements, desired numbers can be easily assigned to the categorical values.

2. Encoding Labels

The technique of converting categorical values in a column to a number is called as "label encoding". Numerical labels always range from "0" to "n categories-1". Encoding a group of categories to a certain numerical value and then encoding all other categories to another numerical value can be done using the *"where()"* function in NumPy. For example, one could encode all the "US airline carriers" to value "1" and all other carriers can be given value "0". You can perform similar label encoding using "Scikit-Learn's LabelEncoder".

Label encoding is fairly intuitive and simple and produces satisfactory performance from your learning algorithm. However, the algorithm is at a disadvantage and may misinterpret numerical values. For example, an algorithm may confuse whether the "U.S. airline carrier" (encoded to 6) should be given 6 times more weight "U.S. airline carrier" (encoded to 1).

3. One-Hot encoding

To resolve the misinterpretation issue of the machine learning algorithm generated by the "label encoding" technique, each categorical data value can be transformed into a new column and that new column can be allocated a '1' or '0' (True/False) value, and is called as "one-hot encoding".

Of all the machine learning libraries in the market that offer "one-hot encoding", the easiest one is *"get_dummies()"* technique in "Pandas", which is appropriately titled given the fact that dummy/indicator data variables such as "1" or "0" are created. In its preprocessing module, Scikit-Learn also supports "one-hot encoding" in its pre-processing module via "LabelBinarizer" and "OneHotEncoder" techniques.

While "one-hot encoding" addresses the issue of misinterpreted category weights, it gives rise to another issue. Creation of multiple new columns to solve this category weight problem for numerous categories can lead to a "curse of dimensionality". The logic behind "curse of dimensionality" is that some equations simply stop functioning correctly in high-dimensional spaces.

4. Binary encoding

This method initially encodes the categories as "ordinal", then converts these integers into a binary string, and then divides digits of that binary code into distinct columns. Therefore, the data is encoded in only a few dimensions, unlike the "one-hot encoding" method.

There are several options to implement binary encoding in your machine learning model but the easiest option is to install "category_encoders" library. This can be done using "pip install category_encoders" on cmd.

5. Backward difference encoding

This "backward difference encoding" method falls within the "contrast coding scheme" for categorical attributes. A "K" category or level characteristic typically enters a "regression" as a series of dummy "K-1" variables. This technique works by drawing a comparison between the "mean" of the dependent variable for a level with the "mean" of the dependent variable in the preceding stage. This kind of encoding is widely used for a "nominal" or an "ordinal "variable".

The code structure for this technique is quite similar to any other technique in the "category_encoders" library, except the run command for this technique is "BackwardDifferenceEncoder".

6. Miscellaneous features

You may sometimes deal with categorical columns that indicate the range of values in observation points, for instance, an 'age' column can contain categories such as '0-20', '20-40', '40-60' etc. While there may be many methods to handle such attributes, the most popular ones are:

Chapter 11: Loading Data, File Formats and Storage

There is not much use of the tools listed in this book if you are unable to perform the data import and export using Python. We will stick to input/output methods related to pandas library only. Although there exist many other tools in various libraries for taking input and providing output such as NumPy.

The main purpose of using input & output in data analysis is to load the data from different databases, read csv text files as well as any other systematic disk format, and to interact with network web application programming interfaces (APIs).

How to Read and Write Data in Text Format

Python is considered a powerful programming language for manipulating text files because of its simple syntax to interact directly with the files, features such as tuple packing/unpacking, and well-built data structures.

There are numerous functions present in pandas library to perform read operation on tabular data. Here is a table listing some of the functions.

Function name	Description of the function
read_csv	It is used to load the data from a file or a URL using a delimiter. It uses comma as the default delimiter.
read_table	It is used to load the data from a file or a URL using a delimiter. It uses tab as the default delimiter.

read_fwf	It is used to read the data, which is present in a fixed width column format having no delimiters in it.
read_clipboard	It is a similar version of data_table. But it doesn't read the data from files and uses the clipboard data for reading purpose. Thus, it comes handy to convert tables present in webpages.

Let us see an overview about how to use the above functions for converting the text file's data into a DataFrame. Here are the options under which the above functions fall:

Date-time parsing: It covers the combining power to combine date and time data present in numerous columns into one sole column while showing the result.

Indexing: It has the capability to use one as well as more than one column while returning the DataFrame. It also has the option to choose or not to choose the column names present in the file.

Iteration: It has the capability to support iteration of a large amount of data present in the large size files.

Data conversion and type inference: It covers personalized list for the value markers, which are not present and conversions related to user defined values.

Skipping data: It includes row, footer, and numeric data skipping from the file.

The most important feature for any function is type inference. By using it, we you don't need to worry about describing the column type like integer, string, boolean, numeric, etc. Let us see one example of csv file (comma separated values).

Let's see an example:

In [154]: !cat chapter05/csvExample1.csv

w, x, y, z, word

10, 20, 30, 40, this

50, 60, 70, 80, is

90, 100, 110, 120, fun

As it is a csv file, we can use the comma as a delimiter and use read_csv function to read the file into a DataFrame.

In [155]: df = pd.read_csv('chapter05/csvExample1.csv')

In [156]: df

Out [156]:

```
    w   x   y   z  word
0  10  20  30  40  this
1  50  60  70  80  is
2  90  100 110 120 fun
```

It can also be done using the read_table function by describing the delimiter.

In [157]: pd.read_table('chapter05/csvExample1.csv', sep=',')

Out [157]:

wxyzword

0   10203040   this

1   50 60 70 80   is

2   90 100 110 120 fun

Note: We have used the cat shell command for printing the contents present in the file. If you are using Unix, and instead using Windows, you need to use the keyword "type" and not "cat" to print it on your screen.

It's not necessary that every file will have a header row. Let's see the below example:

In [158]: !cat chapter05/csvExample2.csv

10, 20, 30, 40, this

50, 60, 70, 80, is

90, 100, 110, 120, fun

We have two options to read this. One is to permit the pandas library to automatically assign the default column names. The other option is to specify the column names on your own.

In [159]: pd.read_csv('chapter05/csvExample2.csv', header = None)

Out [159]:

X.1X.2X.3X.4X.5

0   10203040   this

1   50 60 70 80   is

2   90 100 110 120 fun

In [160]: pd.read_csv('chapter05/csvExample2.csv', names = ['w', 'x', 'y', 'z', 'word'])

Out [160]:

wxyzword

0   10203040   this

1   50   60   70   80   is

2   90   100 110 120 fun

If you want to arrange the values in a hierarchy using multiple columns, you can pass the list of column names or numbers. Here is an example:

In [161]: !cat chapter05/csvExample3.csv

firstKey, secondKey, firstValue, secondValue

one, w, 10, 20

one, x, 30, 40

one, y, 50, 60

one, z, 70, 80

two, w, 90, 100

two, x, 110, 120

two, y, 130, 140

two, z, 150, 160

In [162]: parse_data = pd.read_csv(' chapter05/csvExample3.csv', index_col=[' firstKey ', ' secondKey '])

In [163]: parse_data

Out [163]:

firstValuesecondValue

firstKey secondKey

onew 10 20

x 30 40

y 50 60

z 70 80

two w 90 100

x 110 120

y 130 140

z 150 160

Parser function provides a lot of additional arguments, which can be used to handle many file format exceptions. For example, skiprows allows you to skip any rows present in the text file. Let's see an example:

In [164]: !cat chapter05/csvExample4.csv

Hi!

We are making it a little bit difficult for you

w, x, y, z, word

In today's modern world, you can easily skip any rows present in a file

10, 20, 30, 40, this

50, 60, 70, 80, is

90, 100, 110, 120, fun

In [165]: pd.read_csv(' chapter05/csvExample4.csv', skiprows = [0, 1, 3])

Out [165]:

wxyzword

0 10203040   this

1 50 60 70 80   is

2 90 100 110 120 fun

A very important part in the parsing process, which is commonly used, is "Missing data handling". In these cases, either the missing data is not present in the file or it is marked as a sentinel value. In parsing, pandas use common sentinels like NA, NULL, and -1.

Now let us see an example:

In [166]: !cat chapter05/csvExample5.csv

anyValue , w, x, y, z, word

one, 10, 20, 30, 40, NA

NA, 50, 60 , , 80, is

three, NA, 100, 110, 120, fun

In [167]: final_result = pd.read_csv('chapter05/csvExample5.csv')

In [168]: final_result

Out [168]:

anyValue w x y z word

0 one 10 20 30 40 NaN

1 NaN 50 60 NaN 80 is

2 three NaN 100 110 120 fun

In [169]: pd.isnull(final_result)

Out [169]:

anyValue w x y z word

0 False False False False False True

1 True False False True False False

2 False True False False False False

The option na_values will either take a set of string values or a list while considering the missing values in the text file.

In [170]: final_result = pd.read_csv(' chapter05/csvExample5.csv', na_values = ['NULL'])

In [171]: final_result

Out [171]:

anyValue w x y z word

0 one 10 20 30 40 NaN

1 NaN 50 60 NaN 80 is

2 three NaN 100 110 120 fun

We can specify fifferent NA sentinels for every column present in the text file.

Now let's see an example:

In [172]: sentinels = { 'word': ['fun', 'NA'], 'anyValue': ['one'] }

In [173]: pd.read_csv(chapter05/csvExample5.csv', na_values=sentinels)

Out [173]:

something a b c d message

anyValue w x y z word

0 NaN 10 20 30 40 NaN

1 NaN 50 60 NaN 80 is

2 three NaN 100 110 120 NaN

Argument name	Description of the argument
Path	It is a string value that is used to indicate the location of file, file-like objects, or the URL.
Delimiter or sep	It is used to split the columns present in each row by either using a regular expression or a character sequence.
Names	It is used to show the result in form of column names, combined with the header value as None.
na_values	It is used to provide the sequence of values, which needs to be replaced by NA
Header	It is used to provide the row number that will be used as column names. The default value is 0 and is None in case there is no header row present in the file.
comment	It is used to split the character(s) comments after the end of lines.

date_parser	It is used for parsing dates from a text file.
index_col	It is used to provide the column names or numbers that need to be used as row index in result.
Nrows	It I used to pass the number of rows, which need to be read from the starting point of the file.
Verbose	It is used to print different output information, such as total number of missing values that are present in non-numeric columns.
Iterator	It is used to return the TextParser object to read the file in steps.
convertors	It is used to perform name mapping on functions.
skip_footer	It is used to provide the number of lines, which needs to be ignored at the end of the file.
Squeeze	It is used to return a series if the parsed data has only one column present in it.
chunksize	It is used to iterate and provide size of the file chunks.
encoding	It is used to provide the text encoding for Unicode system.
Dayfirst	It is used to deal with international format when ambiguous dates are getting parsed. Its default value is false.

How to Read Small Pieces of Text Files

In cases where we get huge files having lakhs of rows and columns in it, in order to process the file in the correct format, we need to read small chunks of file by iteration.

Now let us see an example:

In [174]: final_result = pd.read_csv('chapter05/example6.csv')

In [175]: final_result

Out [175]:

<class 'pandas.core.frame.DataFrame'>

Int64Index: 50000 entries, 0 to 49999

Data columns:

w 50000 non-null values

x 50000 non-null values

y 50000 non-null values

z 50000 non-null values

word 50000 non-null values

dtypes: int64(4), object(1)

We can see that this is a very large file having 50,000 rows in it. Therefore, we will read the file in small pieces of rows instead of reading the complete file. It can be done using "nrows".

In [176]: pd.read_csv('chapter05/example6.csv', nrows = 10)

Out [176]:

wxyzword

0 10203040   A

1 50 60 70 80   B

2 90 100 110 120 C

3130140150160D

4170180190200E

510203040F

650607080G

790100110120H

81301401501601

9170180190200J

In order to read the file, we can also use chunksize for number of rows.

In [177]: file_chunker = pd.read_csv('chapter05/example6.csv', chunksize = 500)

In [178]: file_chunker

Out [178]: <pandas.io.parsers.TextParser at 0x8398150>

TextParser object gets returned from read_csv will be iterating the file as per the chunksize fixed above i.e. 500. Therefore, we can aggregate the total value counts in "key" column by iterating the example6 file.

file_chunker = pd.read_csv('chapter05/example6.csv', chunksize = 500)

total = Series([])

for data_piece in file_chunker:

total = total.add(data_piece['key'].value_counts(), fill_value = 0)

total = total.order(ascending = False)

Now we will get the below result:

In [179]: total[:10]

Out [179]:

F 460

Y 452

J 445

P 438

R 429

N 417

K 407

V 400

B 391

D 387

TextParser also has a get_chunk method. It helps us to read the pieces of random size from the file.

How to Write Data Out to Text Format?

We can export data in a delimited format as well by reading it from the csv file. Now let us see an example:

In [180]: final_data = pd.read_csv('chapter05/example5.csv')

In [181]: final_data

Out [181]:

anyValue w x y z word

0 one 10 20 30 40 NaN

1 two 50 60 NaN 80 is

2 three NaN 100 110 120 fun

Now by using the to_csv method found in DataFrame, we can write the resultant data in a comma separated file easily.

In [182]: final_data.to_csv('chapter05/csv_out.csv')

In [183]: !cat chapter05/csv_out.csv

, anyValue, w, x, y, z, word

0, one, 10, 20, 30, 40,

1, two, 50, 60, , 80, is

2, three, 90, 100, 110, 120, fun

You are free to use any other delimiter as well and is not limited to comma only.

In [184]: final_data.to_csv(sys.stdout, sep = '|')

| anyValue| w| x| y| z| word

0| one| 10| 20| 30| 40|

1| two| 50| 60| | 80| is

2| three| 90| 100| 110| 120| fun

All the missing values will show up as empty in the output. You can replace them with any sentinel of your choice.

In [185]: final_data.to_csv(sys.stdout, na_rep = 'NA')

, anyValue, w, x, y, z, word

0, one, 10, 20, 30, 40, NA

1, two, 50, 60, NA, 80, is

2, three, 90, 100, 110, 120, fun

Reading Delimited Formats Manually

By using functions like read_table, we are able to load almost 90% tabular data from the disk. But, in some cases, manual intervention may be required to process the data. We might receive a file that has one or multiple malformed lines that fail the read_table function while loading the data. Now let us see an example:

In [186]: !cat chapter05/example7.csv

"x", "y", "z"

"10", "20", "30", "40"

"10", "20", "30", "40", "50"

We can use Python' built in csv module on order to read a file having only 1-character delimiter in it.

To do so, we need to pass the file to the csv.reader function.

import csv

foo = open('chapter05/example7.csv')

obj_reader = csv.reader(foo)

When we will iterate obj_reader as a field, it will provide the result by removing the quote characters automatically.

In [187]: for line in obj_reader:

.....: print line

['x', 'y', 'z']

['10', '20', '30', '40']

['10', '20', '30', '40', '50']

Now from here, it is your decision to perform wrangling in order to manipulate the data in your own form. Now let us see an example:

In [188]: output_lines = list(csv.reader(open('chapter05/example7.csv')))

In [189]: header, values = output_lines[0], output_lines[1:]

In [190]: obj_dict = { i: v for i, v in zip(header, zip(*values)) }

In [191]: obj_dict

Out [191]: {'x': ('10', '10'), 'y': ('20', '20'), 'z': ('30', '30') }

Comma separated values i.e. cs files have various formats. You can define your own new format having a specific delimiter, line terminator. You simply need to define a subclass of csv.Dialect to achieve this. Here is an example:

```
class own_dialect(csv.Dialect):

line_terminator = '\n'

value_delimiter = ';'

quote_char = '""'

obj_reader = csv.reader(foo, dialect = own_dialect)
```

You can also use dialect parameters directly as keywords and no need to define a subclass.

obj_reader = csv.reader(foo, delimiter = '|')

In order to manually write the delimited files, we can use the csv.writer function. It will accept the same file and dialect options as the csv.reader function. Let's see an example.

with open('delimited_data.csv', 'w') as foo:

obj_writer = csv.writer(foo, dialect = own_dialect)

obj_writer.writerow((x, 'y', 'z'))

obj_writer.writerow(('10', '20', '30'))

obj_writer.writerow(('40', '50', '60'))

Data in Binary Format

The best way to store data safely in the binary format is to use Python's built-in pickle serialization. For your convenience, all objects in pandas provide a save function to write the data as a pickle.

Now let us see an example:

In [192]: obj_frame = pd.read_csv('chapter05/example1.csv')

In [193]: obj_frame

Out [193]:

w, x, y, z, word

10, 20, 30, 40, this

50, 60, 70, 80, is

90, 100, 110, 120, fun

In [194]: obj_frame.save('chapter05/pickle_frame')

We can read back the data into Python using the pandas.load function.

In [195]: pd.load('chapter05/pickle_frame')

Out [195]:

w, x, y, z, word

10, 20, 30, 40, this

50, 60, 70, 80, is

90, 100, 110, 120, fun

Note: You can use pickle only for a short term storage format because it is not 100% guaranteed that the pickle format will be formed and solid with time. A newer version of the library might not unpickle an object that has been pickled today.

Chapter 12: Career Applications

Now then, we've looked over all the skills and libraries you'll need to be proficient in, in order to become a data analyst using python. Naturally, this is merely scratching the surface, we've just gone over the most important facts you need to know before your career gets on the road.

With that being said, you do need to know what that career will be, don't you? Unlike popular belief would suggest, studying data analytics doesn't imply having to bec0me an analyst. In fact, analyzing data is so widespread today that your skillset will be desired almost anywhere.

But let's not get ahead of ourselves here, first let's look at some of the most wanted data analytics related jobs out there:

1. IT Systems Analyst

This is one of the most low-paying jobs you can work as a data analyst. Even then, you'll still typically be seeing figures of around $69,000 a year for your services. This is also very often an excellent entry point to a company, because too many people higher up, you'll just sound like "The IT guy" giving you more vertical mobility because you'll be less shackled to a particular niche.

The level of knowledge you'll have to possess before you become one of these will vary depending on the company. To explain how vague this job is, think about a job posting in 2019 asking for a "computer programmer," sure you might know how to program computers, but you might not know the languages or frameworks the company uses. Because of this, it's only advisable to apply for these jobs if you're absolutely sure about what the company is doing.

Sometimes, you'll be using Python, like you've been taught in this book. other times, you might be using the third-party software, or even be tasked with software testing and development. You might also have to make your own tools, although this would command a higher pay(or at last, you should ask for it, as they won't be finding many competent people at 69 grand a year.)

2. Healthcare Data Analyst

This is quite self-explanatory; you analyze health data. While the job sounds simple, it's actually quite challenging, interesting, and like many positions in the health industry: underpaid. At only about $62,000 a year, it is by far the lowest-paid position on this list.

On the bright side, you'll be tasked with researching new methods to improve the lives of countless people. You'll be working with some of the brightest minds in medical science trying to solve problems they couldn't.

There's also a ton of data in the healthcare industry. If you're very set on working with technical data analytics, and your soft skills are lacking, then this position might be for you. With so many data points, provided by things like smartwatches and smartphones running calculators, you'll be hard-pressed to find a field with more available data.

While the position is currently not paid very well in the US, this is promising to change. With many different laws coming out that govern how data is handled, the need for a competent data analyst also skyrockets.

3. Operations Analyst

As an operations analyst, you'll mostly be working at large companies, though if you've proved yourself enough, it might be advisable to freelance or open a consulting firm.

Now, the average salary for an operations analyst is $75 000 a year, making it quite well paid. It is worth keeping in mind, though, that this statistic includes all operations analysts, which are found in, well, everything. Military, food services, banks, everyone has a need for an internal data analyst.

If you want to be an internal part of a business's success, then the job of an operations analyst might be for you. You'll find that you're handling people almost as much as data. You'll be tasked with making reporting systems, as well as analyzing the efficiency of the business's internal operations such as manufacturing and distributing goods.

In this position, it's extremely important to be well-versed in business. While you'll need to have high-level knowledge of the systems you're using, none of that means anything unless you know how to apply it to practical, business matters.

4. Data Scientist

Data scientist, at this point, has become more of a buzzword than an actual job. While yes, you'll be collecting and analyzing data in order to get to a result, generally, you'll be seen as above a data analyst. While an analyst analyzes low-level data and applies it to a business's internal workings, a scientist doesn't tend to bother with that. You'll be tasked with dealing with the theoretical properties of the data and looking at the big picture.

This is where your programming and data visualization skills really pay off. These positions are extremely intensive when it comes to the level of technical knowledge needed to perform them successfully. You'll need to have a very firm grasp of the exact technical specifications of the tools and languages you're using. Unfortunately, this book doesn't cover quite enough to qualify you, but the 2nd and 3rd of the series will do just fine.

If you're looking for a challenging position which will push your capabilities to their limits, then this may be the position for you. The average salary of a data analyst is about $91,000 and is only trending upwards. With the average salary being almost 6 digits, you can probably picture how much the higher-level ones do.

If you're looking to become a data scientist, you'll need a bit more than Python. Looking past it, and checking out technical tutorials on other languages and frameworks would be a great idea. Having a firm grasp of at least one server-side language like SQL, and a functional one like Haskell would be ideal.

5. Data Engineer

Being a data engineer essentially hinges on how well you're able to optimize the large datasets you're given and apply them to a practical situation.

Here, your theoretical knowledge is a slave to the practicalities. If something is impractical, it's useless, no matter how pretty the data might look. For example, you might be analyzing data concerning water flow in a city, checking out how many leeks per cubic meter of piping there is, etc. Then you'd apply the analysis in order to figure out how to best make a very efficient pipeline.

Naturally, this position is more prevalent in the tech industry. There, you'll be looking at acquisition pipelines, as well as speeding up the queries which are given by a set database.

Alongside pretty much every other professional position that has the word "engineer" in it, data engineers are paid very well, with the average pay being about the same as a data analyst.

Despite the two jobs being at completely opposite ends of the theoretical-practical scale, they both command a large payment due to the amount of understanding required to perform them effectively.

6. Quantitative Analyst

Here's another extremely viable position. Quantitative analysts are mostly employed in the field of finance. There, you'll be tasked with dealing with data analytics in order to predict financial movements, manage risks, and find good opportunities for your company to invest in.

This puts you at a very central role in the firm. Hence the median salary for this position is also quite high. While the average pay is around $83,000, that isn't where the true earning potential of this position kicks in.

The actual earning potential from becoming a quantitative analyst derives itself from the fact you'll be able to create your own models for predicting the movement of the financial market. Stocks, cryptocurrency, international bonds, you name it. You might even be able to open your own firm!

7. Data Analytics Consultant

Now, this role is one that's extremely variable. While the median salary is about 80 grand, you'll find that it varies extremely. You'll find one consultant working at well over 6 figures, while another is barely hitting above half the median.

Your role as a consultant will be to give your company valuable insight into what is going on with their data. In this position, it's very important to specialize. Pick a niche and stick to it; this field rewards those that stick to their guns for a long time.

The job description may sound quite similar to a data analyst, and well, it's pretty much the same job. The main difference is that consultants tend to be independent freelancers, and are employed on a contractual basis. This means your career mobility will increase, but job security is near nonexistent.

On the other hand, this position lets you work for multiple companies at a time. This helps quite a bit, as getting fired from a gig won't leave you unemployed all of a sudden.

If you like changing jobs every so often and are fine with grabbing a niche and sticking to it, then consider this position. It's an excellent position for everyone sick and tired of the traditional office environment. Working remotely is also a thing to consider, as it's very easy to work from anywhere in the world as a consultant.

8. Digital Marketing Manager

Now, this is a bit of an unorthodox one. Despite popular belief insisting managers never do anything, data analytics is slowly becoming expected of anyone trying to enter the field of digital marketing. If you've got more skills than just analytics, then you might just be right for a position like this. The most important part of this position is to have a large, varied skill set.

Simply being able to code Python won't suffice here. You'll need to have managerial skills, soft skills, as well as some necessary business knowledge.

In this field, you'll often be using third-party apps such as Google Analytics to provide you with data. Naturally, some firms will use their own tools, or even different third-party ones in order to figure out the spread of their traffic from all of their sources. While all of this requires you to have excellent data analytics skills, you'll later have to delegate this information to a team. Because of this, it's to learn to communicate complex computer-related topics to a non-tech-savvy audience.

Businesses spend a lot of money on advertisements. Billions are thrown around every year into failed marketing attempts. In an effort to prevent this from happening, many of the world's biggest businesses have been employing analysts as managers.

Much like most other managerial positions, this one has a very high average pay, but also quite a large spread. With that being said, with the median yearly salary being $97, 000, you'll be hard-pressed to not get a well-paying job at the least.

9. Project Manager

Being a project manager tends to require quite a bit less skill than being a digital marketing manager, but even so, it's a position which has had steadily increasing requirements.

Currently, a top project manager would be expected to use multiple analytics tools to determine how well their team is performing. With a median salary of around $73, 000, it's not half bad for so much work.

In this role, since you'll be managing a team, your data analytics skills will have to take a back seat to more people-oriented soft skills. With that being said, you'll run into a lot of situations where these skills will help you.

If you hate working at big firms, then this position isn't for you. This is mostly because project managers are generally only needed when the magnitude of the company is large enough for them to be unable to delegate managerial duties to the managers higher up. Project managers have some decent vertical mobility, though, with an almost clear path to a supply chain manager, which rakes in quite a bit more money.

10. Transportation Logistics Specialist

Here's quite an interesting area. As a transportation logistics specialist, you'll be trying to best figure out transport! This can be the transport of anything, ranging from the transport of healing stones from Amazon to the transport of foreign ministers. You'll be dealing with some really important things in this position.

Having a solid background in data analytics isn't necessary for this job. With that being said, it's extremely helpful; the job will demand you to be capable of determining the most efficient way to transport goods. This can be hard to do without the necessary skills to look at a lot of data and figure out where the bottlenecks are. After that, it'll be up to you to figure out how to solve them.

An average salary you can expect to get is about $79, 000 a year. Which isn't too bad, especially for such an entertaining job. If you're able to think closely about minute details, and are good at handling technicalities and thinking in advance, then you might find that being a transportation logistics specialist is ideal for you.

Sidenotes:

We've only looked at data in the United States for these examples. The pay scales may vary in your country or even city. With that being said, most jobs in data analytics are dependant on the local economy. For example, in the US, Boston, and Portland are much better for a data analytic than, say, New Mexico.

An excellent thing about being a data scientist outside of the US is that you can still have a US salary. The US has some of the highest costs of living in the world, so if you're living in a cheaper nation, and working remotely, you'll be living the lavish lifestyle of your dreams in no time.

Jobs in data analytics tend to be highly competitive salary-wise anyways, and this is only further intensified by your decreased cost of living.

Now, let us consider a unique occupation, seldom found in many other fields:

Freelancing

Data analytics has a near-endless amount of freelancing and remote positions available to it. While we've already looked at the potential that remote work offers, if your skills are sharp enough, then your career will prosper most as a freelancer.

You're probably already aware, but freelancing is essentially remote contract work. You reach out to clients yourself and try to get them to hire you. The best thing about being a freelancer is that you're your own boss, never will anyone be able to dictate your wages, or fire you.

Sure, you might lose a project or two, but that's the beauty of it, you can take on as much work as you're capable of doing. This makes the work culture much easier to enjoy.

Think about others working 8 hours a day, 4 of those 8 hours are probably spent rather uselessly. On the other hand, as a freelancer, all of the time you spend "at work" will be spent working and earning money.

This makes freelancing very appealing to those people that take a lot of pride into their work. After all, all of your work will stand as a testament to your skills.

Freelancing probably isn't the best way to kickstart your career, as without a portfolio you'll have a lot of difficulties securing jobs. On the other hand, if you've got an extensive portfolio, freelancing might be just the thing for you.

When it comes to median wages, it's almost impossible to figure out for freelancers. After all, anyone can charge whatever they want. On the other hand, for the top brass of freelancers, pay rates such as $100 per hour are nowhere near unheard of. Some of them, on platforms such as UpWork, make over $250 an hour for consulting services.

There are two main ways to approach a freelancing career. The first is to send out emails to companies and startups you think need your services, networking helps a lot in this. Attend events and advertise your services wherever you can.

Trying to attend startup events is great in this case, you might even approach companies in person and share your details so they may call upon your services.

The reason freelancing is at the bottom of these occupations is that, well, it's hardly an occupation. Freelancing is more akin to running your own business. You have to be your own PR, your own marketing, and your own boss. All of this responsibility can be quite hard to shoulder for anyone. You'll need to excel at all of these areas to make your presence known.

It's important to gather testimonials from past clients; everyone you've ever worked for is a valuable asset in getting more work set out. This is why, as a freelancer, it's extremely important to get a wide network of satisfied clients.

On the other hand, you have the path of using aggregate sites like UpWork as your source of work. If you haven't heard of these previously, they basically let you find freelance work through the freelance equivalent of a traditional job board.

These job boards have both pros and

Conclusion

Thank you for making it through to the end. The next step is to start looking at some of the different methods that can be used to help you to analyze any kind of data that you have available and put it to good use for your own needs. Many businesses are going to be able to gather a lot of data, but it is what we do with the data that is really going to matter. If you do not use the data in the proper manner, and you just let it sit there, then you are not going to gain the competitive edge that you want. And this is where the data analysis is going to come into play.

Data analysis lets us know the patterns that are in our data and helps us to work on what is inside of the data that we have gathered. This can be used to make better business decisions, helps to provide better customer service, and so much more. And the different libraries and techniques that are used in this guidebook will help us to learn the exact steps that we need to follow in order to get this data analysis done.

There are a lot of different things that we discussed in this guidebook concerning data analysis and how we can perform our own analysis with the help of the Python language. Some of the topics to remember in the review include:

A look at what data analysis is all about and why you would want to use it.

How to get your Python environment set up with all of the libraries we are going to use in this guidebook.

A bit about the SciPy library and how it works.

What the NumPy library is able to bring to the table and why you would want to use it.

The Pandas library and how it is different from some of the others in helping you with data analysis.

How to do data wrangling with Pandas

Data visualization and a look at the Matplotlib library.

How to use Matplotlib to create some of your own plots and get started with your own data analysis.

A look at what data analysis is all about and why you would want to use it.

How to get your Python environment set up with all of the libraries we are going to use in this guidebook.

A bit about the SciPy library and how it works.

What the NumPy library is able to bring to the table and why you would want to use it.

The Pandas library and how it is different from some of the others in helping you with data analysis.

How to do data wrangling with Pandas

Data visualization and a look at the Matplotlib library.

How to use Matplotlib to create some of your own plots and get started with your own data analysis.

There are many times when creating our own analysis can help. Companies know the value of collecting data, but the data analysis actually puts that information to use. This guidebook has provided you with the information you need to really see success with your own data analysis today!

www.ingramcontent.com/pod-product-compliance
Lightning Source LLC
Chambersburg PA
CBHW071141050326
40690CB00008B/1531